THE HOODOO ROSARY

The Hoodoo Rosary

Anielle Reid

Contents

Dedication	viii
Preface: My Path to the Hoodoo Rosary	xi
Introduction	xiii
1 What is Hoodoo?	1
2 Who is the Virgin Mother Mary in Hoodoo?	4
3 What is the Rosary?	9
4 How do you Pray the Rosary?	13
5 What are the Rosary Prayers Exactly?	18
The Our Father	21
Hail Mary	25
Glory Be	29
Fatima Prayer	32
6 What are the Rosary's Mysteries?	36
7 The Joyful Mysteries	40
The Annunciation	42
The Visitation	46
The Nativity	49

The Presentation in the Temple	52
The Finding in the Temple	56
8 The Sorrowful Mysteries	59
The Scourging	62
The Agony in the Garden	65
Crowning with Thorns	68
The Carrying of the Cross	71
The Crucifixion and Death of Jesus	74
9 The Glorious Mysteries	77
Resurrection	79
The Ascension	82
The Descent of the Holy Spirit	85
The Assumption of Mary	88
The Coronation of Mary	92
10 The Luminous Mysteries	95
The Baptism	97
The Wedding at Cana	100
The Proclamation of the Kingdom	104
The Transfiguration	108
The Eucharist	111
11 Praying the Rosary with Intention	114
12 The Rosary as a Magical Tool	118
13 Working the Rosary	123
14 Praying the Rosary for Specific Needs	127
Money Drawing & Abundance Rosary	130

Power and Command Rosary	137
Protection Rosary	143
Road-Opener Rosary	149
Romantic Rosary	155
Uncrossing Rosary	160
The Hoodoo Mysteries	166
15 What You Can Expect from the Hoodoo Rosary Path	176
16 Living the Prayer	183
The Traditional Mysteries with Scripture	186
The Seven Joys of Mary Rosary	192
The Seven Sorrows of Mary Rosary	195
The Psalms and the Mysteries	199
Marian Feast Days	203
Popular Marian Prayers	206
Marian Titles	211
Christian Ancestors & Spiritual Lineage	215
Frequently Asked Questions About the Rosary	220
About the Author	226

To Mary, the Ancestors, and the Spirits
Who Pray With Us and For Us

Copyright © 2025 by Danielle Reid

All rights reserved. No part of this book may be reproduced in any manner whatsoever without written permission except in the case of brief quotations embodied in critical articles and reviews.

First Printing, 2025

Preface: My Path to the Hoodoo Rosary

I was born into two worlds — one of spirit, and one of prayer.

As a child, I saw my grandfather frequently after his passing, not knowing he was the one who had brought Catholicism into our family. I dreamed dreams that carried messages for others. I didn't know the word conjure, but it was already alive in me.

Catholicism was always in the background — Catholic school, Hail Marys, my grandmother watching *The Song of Bernadette* — but I never called myself Catholic. I carried both the gospel rhythms of my grandmother's Sunday radio and the unseen world that visited me in dreams.

It wasn't until I embraced my work as a medium in 2018 that I met a Christian ancestor, a Celtic monk, who taught me the psalms and how they could be used in magic. But it was during my pregnancy and early motherhood that I truly felt Christianity calling me. I could feel Mary's presence, gentle yet insistent, reaching for me. The rosary found me again — or maybe it was I who found it — as I became a mother. With a newborn in my arms, long rituals were no longer possible, but the beads were. I could hold them, pray, and meditate on the mysteries while nursing or during contact naps.

The rosary became my bridge: between motherhood and magic, Catholic mysticism and Hoodoo, spirit and lineage.

The Hoodoo Rosary isn't just a set of prayers — it's my craft, my connection to my ancestors, and one of my ways of touching the divine. It's how I honor the interwoven paths of faith, spirit, and motherhood that brought me to this moment.

Introduction

The Hoodoo Rosary is the rosary reimagined — a devotion, a meditative practice, and a tool for manifestation. It embraces the syncretism of Catholicism so deeply woven into the spiritual lives of many within the African Diaspora, using the rosary as a sacred technology for magic.

While the rosary itself is a chaplet, in this work the term Hoodoo Rosary is expansive. It includes not only the five-decade Marian rosary, but also other chaplets: the St. Michael Chaplet, the St. Anne Chaplet, the Seven Sorrows of Mary, and the Seven Joys of Mary. Each can be used within Hoodoo practice, though the foundation remains the Marian Psalter — the five-decade rosary — whose mysteries align beautifully with the psalms. And the psalms, as any rootworker knows, are central in Hoodoo prayerwork.

The Hoodoo Rosary is part of a long tradition within the African Diaspora of incorporating magic under the cover of Catholic devotion — and also of reclaiming Catholic mysticism for what it is: a rich, symbolic, and potent system of spiritual technology. The rosary is not only a path to Mary's heart but a pathway into the soul's own mysteries, an engine for focused prayer, and a vessel for intention.

When you begin to pray the rosary — to meditate on its mysteries, to feel the beads moving through your fingers — the magic will unveil itself to you. And when you consciously work the rosary through a Hoodoo lens, you'll see how this simple strand of beads can connect you to your ancestors, to your magic, and to the deepest truths of your own spirit.

1

What is Hoodoo?

Hoodoo is African American folk magic.

It is the spiritual child of survival, resistance, and deep-rooted ancestral wisdom. Born from the blending of African traditions, Indigenous knowledge, and European influences, Hoodoo is not one single system—it is a living practice, shaped by the hands, hearts, and spirits of those who carried it through centuries of struggle and creativity.

At its root, Hoodoo is African. It came to the Americas in the hearts and memories of the enslaved, carried in song, story, prayer, and in the quiet work of roots and hands. On the New World's soil, it met the plant medicine and sacred ways of Indigenous peoples, and the tools and folk customs of Europeans. Out of necessity, it adapted—using whatever was available, transforming everyday items into magical tools.

Hoodoo is often called rootwork because of its traditional use of herbs, roots, and natural curios, but it is more than that. You can be a "rootworker" without ever touching a plant. Hoodoo is also prophetic dreams. It is speaking blessings—or curses—with your mouth. It is signs, omens, and gestures passed down without explanation. It is knowing you do not put your purse on the floor, even if no one can tell you why. It is the unspoken magic that lives in our blood and in our habits.

For African Americans, Hoodoo is a birthright. Many believe that if you carry African American blood, you can do Hoodoo—there is no initiation beyond being born into it. But Hoodoo also has a broader face, one that can be embraced by people of all backgrounds who respect its history and spirit. At its heart, Hoodoo is folk magic, a syncretic practice that gathers what works—from wherever it comes—and makes it your own.

Because of the danger faced by our ancestors, much of Hoodoo has always been hidden. During slavery, it was not safe to be openly practicing African religion, so the Bible became both a shield and a sword. It was a cover that allowed our people to pray their own way, speak their own blessings, and work their own magic while appearing to conform to Christianity. Over time, the Bible itself became an integral part of Hoodoo—not as an imposed text, but as a powerful magical book, full of Psalms and stories that carry spells, blessings, and divine authority.

I am African, Indigenous, and European. Hoodoo teaches me to embrace all that I am—to claim every ancestor, every tradition, and every gift that flows through my veins. In this book, you will find me making allusion to one of my European ancestors often, because Hoodoo is about wholeness. It is about weaving together every thread of who we are into a living tapestry of magic.

Hoodoo is survival magic.

It is faith magic.

It is blood magic.

And in The Hoodoo Rosary, it is a path that invites Mary, the saints, the angels, and the ancestors into your work—because in Hoodoo, we use what is given to us, and we make it holy.

2

Who is the Virgin Mother Mary in Hoodoo?

Mary has always found her way into the conjure room.

For some within the African Diaspora, she arrived as the white Virgin Mother presented by Christian missionaries; for others, she was already known through the Ethiopian Bible; for still others, she was syncretized with Yemaya, carried on the waves of ancestral memory. She appears in many faces: Queen of Angels, Our Lady of Perpetual Help, Mother of Sorrows, Star of the Sea. In Brazil, she is Nossa Senhora Aparecida; in Cuba, she is Our Lady of Charity of El Cobre who is syncretized with the orisha Ochun. She is the Black Madonna, the divine feminine archetype, the Theotokos for some, and simply "Mary, the mother of Jesus" for others.

In Catholicism and Hoodoo, Mary's identity shifts depending on who is calling her and for what purpose. Yet in magic, she is more than a saint — she is a powerful spiritual ally. In my own practice, Mary has given me a conscientious understanding of Christ and what it means in the literal sense as "anointed." As much as I hate to admit it, she has proven the old Catholic saying "to Christ through Mary" true. It is through working with her that I gained a deeper understanding of the Christ within and what that energy truly represents. Through Mary, I have come to see the true symbology and mysticism embedded within Christian texts, unlocking meanings I had previously overlooked.

Mary has also awakened my maternal energy, refining the traits and graces I need as a mother: acceptance, patience, presence, and the understanding that suffering, too, has its reasons.

Her biblical life story — as told in scripture and in apocryphal texts like the Protoevangelium of James — mirrors the experiences of many in the Diaspora: endurance through hardship, displacement, danger, and yet carrying the seed of promise.

To me, she represents hope, our potential and the "Mary" that exists within all of us. As Neville Goddard taught, we can all become Mary, as she symbolizes the womb of creation—our imagination. "The virgin mother Mary is the personification of your own imagination, which gives birth to the Savior," Goddard said. Mary represents the creative power within us, the ability to imagine and bring forth a new reality.

And in addition to that, within my own life Mary is a literal being and a deity, a Queen of Angels who can introduce you to other angelic forces. She has deepened my work as a psychopomp, a guide of souls to the afterlife, for she is well-known among the devout as one who promises to be present at the hour of death. Tradition holds that those who faithfully pray the rosary will see her face at death and be granted a holy passing.

Mary's presence is felt not only at literal death but in every kind of transition: at the birth of life, as seen in the Annunciation, at its end, standing at the foot of the cross, and in its complete transformation at the resurrection. She accompanies us through the death of the ego before transformation, the death of an old life before the birth of a new self, and every moment of profound change.

From my work with her, I have learned that the Hail Mary can guide a soul through many crossings, on both sides of the veil. That alone may be one of the many reasons why she is called upon.

In the conjure room, Mary may be called upon with offerings, petitions, and devotional prayers. Popular offerings to Mary include candles (especially blue or white), flowers like roses, carnations or lilies, holy water, and sacred medals or rosaries. To petition her, practitioners often recite the Hail Mary or specific novenas, place written petitions beneath her statue or image, and light candles dedicated to their intention. Some also create altars adorned with her iconography to focus their prayers and devotion. Rootworkers know that she presents herself in a myriad of ways and each of her faces, each of her titles, not only allude to her universality but speak to her intercessory powers. For example, she can come to you as **Our Lady of Perpetual Help** if you are in urgent needs **or as Our Lady, Star of the Sea** if you are lost **or even Our Lady of Sorrows** if you are in grief or trial

But she can be seen in all her glory and do far more when you truly know her story — who she was to Jesus as a mother, who she was as a daughter to St. Anne, a wife to St. Joseph and, in mystical and Gnostic circles, who she was as a vessel of Sophia's wisdom or, as some say, a student of Isis herself.

To work with Mary through Hoodoo is to embrace her as a living, responsive spirit — one who welcomes flowers and cakes, candles and coins, psalms and rosaries. She is the Mother who listens, the Queen who intercedes, and the bridge between the seen and unseen worlds.

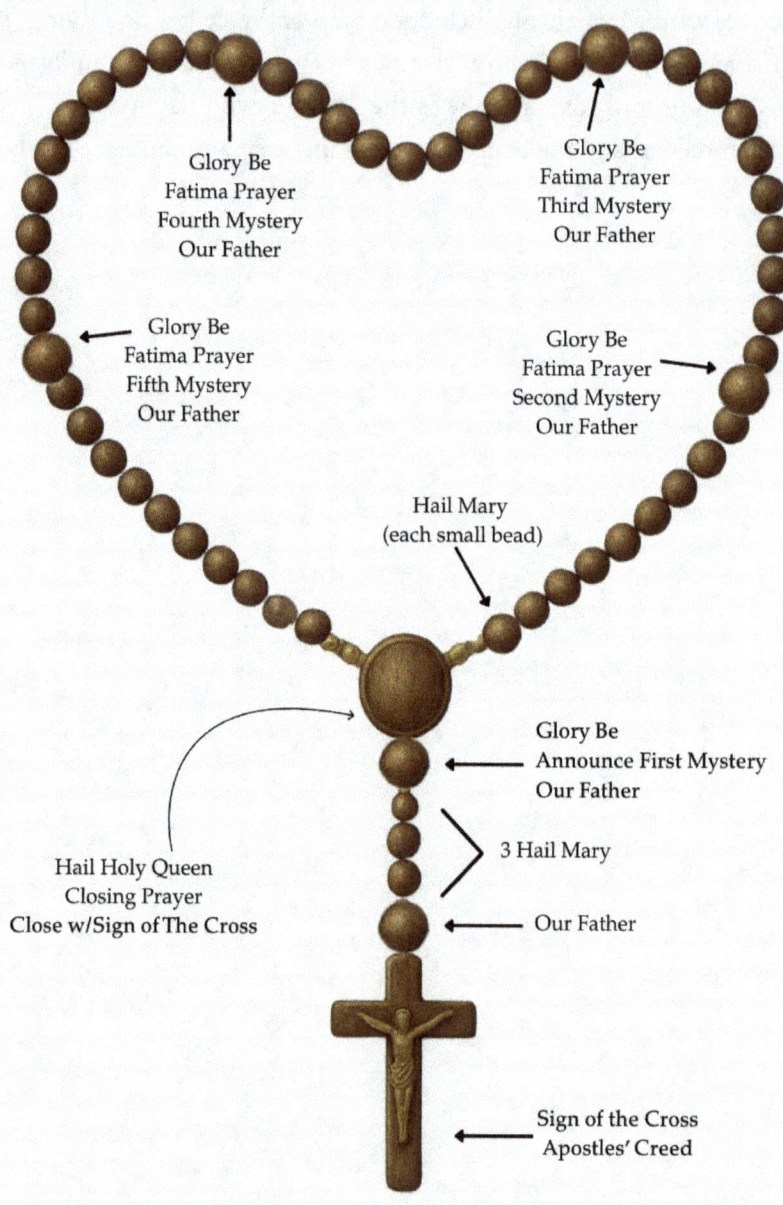

3

What is the Rosary?

The rosary is more than a string of beads—it is a sacred tool, a prayer rope, a spiritual weapon, and a bridge between worlds.

In Catholic tradition, it is believed that the Virgin Mary herself gave the rosary to St. Dominic in the 13th century as a way to fight heresy and call people back to prayer. Whether you believe in that story literally or see it as a vision rich with symbolism, the truth remains: the rosary has been, for centuries, a lifeline for the faithful.

A rosary can be made from anything—wood, crystal, glass, seeds, stone, shells, even water from holy springs set in resin. It can be simple or ornate, humble or luxurious. Some are handcrafted with gemstones for their spiritual correspondences—rose quartz for love, amethyst for spiritual vision, tiger's eye for protection. They come in every color you can imagine, each one carrying the intention of the maker and the devotion of the one who prays on it.

Some people say you should never wear a rosary around your neck. Others, especially in folk tradition, see it as a talisman—a necklace of prayer and power, something that protects you simply by being near your body. Whether worn, held, kept in your pocket, or hung in your home, the rosary carries the energy of the prayers spoken through it. You'll see rosaries draped over rearview mirrors, tucked under pillows, hanging on doorknobs, and even appearing in films—sometimes as a symbol of holiness, sometimes as a symbol of mystery.

The power of the rosary comes from many places. It holds the energy of the one praying it. It holds the weight of centuries of devotion. It holds the power of Jesus, the wisdom of the Scriptures, and the tenderness of Mary. Each bead walks you through moments in the lives of Mary and Jesus—known as the Mysteries—and together they form what is called the Marian Psalter.

It is also a vessel for ancient prayers. The Our Father, the Hail Mary, the Glory Be, and the Hail, Holy Queen are not just words—they are keys. They open doors to deeper parts of yourself. They invite angels, saints, and holy powers into your life. They activate the soul. They can teach you about the art of manifestation itself: focusing the heart, speaking your desire, aligning with divine will, and allowing miracles to unfold.

For some, the rosary has been called Mary's lasso—a cord she throws to catch and save you. I believe it is that, but I also believe it is a rope that pulls you inward, into the depths of your own soul, and upward, toward the heights of Heaven, the Kingdom within. It is both anchor and lifeline.

The rosary is a way to connect with Mary, to commune with angels, to converse with the saints, and to touch the spirit world—but also to journey deep within yourself. It is prayer you can hold in your hands. And when you pray it, you are never alone—Mary prays with you, for you, and around you, wrapping you in the embrace of her unending love.

HOW TO PRAY THE ROSARY

① SIGN OF THE CROSS
In the Name of the Father and of the Son and of the Holy Spirit

② APOSTLE'S CREED
I believe in God, the Father Almighty, Creator of Heaven and Earth...

③ OUR FATHER
who art in Heaven, hallowed be Thy name. Thy Kingdom come, Thy will be done...

④ HAIL MARY
Full of Grace, The Lord is with Thee...

⑤ GLORY BE
to the Father, and to the Son, and to the Holy Spirit as it was in the beginning, is now, and ever shall be, world without end. Amen.

⑥ FATIMA PRAYER
(optional)
O My Jesus, forgive us our sins, save us ...

⑦ HAIL HOLY QUEEN

4

How do you Pray the Rosary?

Below is the traditional structure of the 5 decade Marian rosary along with its prayers, infused with mystical meanings so that you know both what to say to pray the rosary and why it works magically.

1. Sign of the Cross

With clean hands hold the crucifix and make the Sign of the Cross, touching your forehead as you say "In the name of the Father," your chest as you say "and of the Son," and your left and right shoulders as you say "and of the Holy Spirit. Amen."

Mystical Meaning: Creates a protective circle of divine authority. In hoodoo, this is your spiritual warding — calling in the Trinity as guardians of your space.

2. Apostles' Creed

While holding the crucifix in a rested position say "I believe in God, the Father Almighty, Creator of heaven and earth, and in Jesus Christ, His only Son, our Lord, who was conceived by the Holy Spirit, born of the Virgin Mary, suffered under Pontius Pilate, was crucified, died, and was buried. He descended into hell; on the third day, He rose again from the dead; He ascended into heaven and is seated at the right hand of God, the Father Almighty; from there He will come to judge the living and the dead. I believe in the Holy Spirit, the Holy Catholic Church, the communion of saints, the forgiveness of sins, the resurrection of the body, and life everlasting. Amen."

Mystical Meaning: Affirms your spiritual lineage and authority. In magical work, affirmations are power — this creed declares who you are aligned with before entering the spiritual "courtroom."

3. Our Father (The Lord's Prayer)

Move your fingers to the first bead after the crucifix and say "Our Father, who art in heaven, hallowed be Thy name. Thy kingdom come, Thy will be done, on earth as it is in heaven. Give us this day our daily bread, and forgive us our trespasses, as we forgive those who trespass against us. And lead us not into temptation, but deliver us from evil.*"

You may conclude with "Amen" here or, if you prefer, add the optional ending:

"For Thine is the kingdom, and the power, and the glory, forever. Amen."

Mystical Meaning: This is the Master Key. In hoodoo terms, it opens the gate to the Heavenly Court, granting your petition audience before God. It sets the "command" tone.

4. Hail Mary

Move your fingers to the first of three small beads after the Our Father bead and pray "Hail Mary, full of grace, The Lord is with Thee. Blessed art Thou amongst women and blessed is the fruit of Thy Womb, Jesus. Holy Mary, Mother of God, Pray for us Sinners, Now and at the hour of our death. Amen."

Mystical Meaning: This is the invocation of and petition for Mother Mary. She is the one who grants favor and intercedes on behalf of her people. Saying it repeatedly builds rhythm, energy, and connection.

* * *

You will say 1 Hail Mary for each of the 3 Hail Mary beads following the Our Father Bead of the ladder of the rosary. The first is said for an increase in Faith, the second is said for an increase in Hope and the third is said for an increase in Charity.

* * *

5. Glory Be

Move your fingers to the Our Father bead before the center Medallion and say "Glory be to the Father, and to the Son, and to the Holy Spirit, as it was in the beginning, is now, and ever shall be, world without end. Amen."

Mystical Meaning: This seals a petition with praise, which in hoodoo magnifies the outcome. Praise energy is attractive energy — it pulls blessings toward you.

Move your fingers to the Center Medallion and recite your Opening Prayer if applicable, then announce the first Mystery.

To announce the First Mystery you will state it along with its applicable Scripture and then you will advance along the rosary by praying the Our Father prayer, the Hail Mary prayer on each of the 10 Hail Mary Beads while reflecting on the mystery.

When you fingers touch the Our Father bead at the end of the decade you will pray the Glory Be prayer and the optional Fatima Prayer.

6. Fatima Prayer (optional)

With your hands on the Our Father bead say "O My Jesus, forgive us our sins, save us from the fires of Hell and lead all souls to Heaven, especially those who are in most need of Thy mercy."

Mystical Meaning: Acts as a cleansing wash — removing spiritual residue that could hinder your petition's manifestation.

You will repeat steps 3-6 for each of the remaining decades (groups of 10 Hail Mary beads) until you reach the Center Medallion.

7. Hail Holy Queen

With your fingers on the Center Medallion say "Hail, holy Queen, Mother of mercy, hail, our life, our sweetness and our hope. To thee do we cry, poor banished children of Eve: to thee do we send up our sighs, mourning and weeping in this vale of tears. Turn then, most gracious Advocate, thine eyes of mercy toward us, and after this our exile, show unto us the blessed fruit of thy womb, Jesus, O merciful, O loving, O sweet Virgin Mary! Amen."

Mystical Meaning: This is your closing royal address, returning to Mary with gratitude and trust. It completes the magical "circuit."

To conclude you can say an additional Closing Prayer of your choice with your fingers embracing the Center Medallion

Practical Hoodoo Tips While Praying

Anointing: Dress your rosary with an appropriate oil for your intention.

Crystals: Use beads of specific stones (rose quartz for love, citrine for money, black tourmaline for protection).

Candles: Light a color corresponding to your work — green for prosperity, white for peace, red for passion, purple for mastery.

Petition Paper: Keep your petition folded beneath your rosary as you pray.

Timing: Pray during planetary hours or on feast days for added power.

When prayed in this way, the rosary becomes more than devotion — it becomes a conjure tool, a charm, and a living current of divine magic flowing through your words and hands.

5

What are the Rosary Prayers Exactly?

The Rosary is more than just a circle of beads — it is a rhythm of sacred words that carry centuries of devotion, wisdom, and spiritual power. These prayers are the heartbeat of the Rosary, each one chosen and preserved for the way it speaks to God, to Mary, and to the soul of the person praying.

Some of these prayers are ancient, found in Scripture itself. Others are devotional compositions that have been prayed by countless faithful across generations. Together, they form a powerful sequence — a litany of praise, petition, thanksgiving, and surrender — that can lift the spirit, protect the heart, and deepen your connection with the Divine.

In this chapter, I will not only share the traditional wording of these prayers but also open up their deeper layers: the Hoodoo perspective, my own mystical insights, and ways you can use them as living tools for transformation. My goal is to show you that these words are not just recitations, but keys — keys that unlock doors within yourself, within the spirit world, and within the unseen currents of life.

The Core Prayers of the Rosary Are:

1. **The Sign of the Cross** – The sealing prayer that calls on the Holy Trinity and creates a spiritual boundary.

2. **The Apostles' Creed** – A declaration of faith rooted in the earliest Christian tradition.

3. **The Our Father (The Lord's Prayer)** – Given to us by Jesus Himself, a prayer of alignment with Divine will and provision.

4. **The Hail Mary** – A greeting and petition to the Mother of God, rooted in Scripture and in the Church's devotional life.

5. **The Glory Be** – A short hymn of praise to the Trinity.

6. **The Fatima Prayer** – A plea for mercy and salvation for all souls, taught by Mary at Fatima.

7. **The Hail Holy Queen** – A prayer of trust and appeal to Mary's intercession as our Mother and Advocate.

In the pages that follow, we will go through each of these prayers in detail — their history, their meaning, and how they can be used both in devotion and in spiritual work. Some of what I share will be rooted in tradition; other parts will be my own personal revelations and the lived experience of my Hoodoo practice.

By the end of this chapter, my hope is that you will not only understand what these prayers say but how they work — and how they can work for you.

The Our Father

Traditional Text

Our Father, who art in heaven, hallowed be Thy name.

Thy Kingdom come, Thy will be done, on earth as it is in heaven.

Give us this day our daily bread, and forgive us our trespasses, as we forgive those who trespass against us.

And lead us not into temptation, but deliver us from evil. Amen.

Traditional Catholic Perspective

The Our Father is considered by Catholics the perfect prayer, because it was given directly by Jesus when His disciples asked Him how to pray (Matthew 6:9–13, Luke 11:2–4). It is both a prayer of praise and petition.

"Our Father who art in heaven" — Acknowledges God as Father, establishing a relationship of love and trust.

"Hallowed be Thy name" — A prayer of reverence, honoring the holiness of God's name.

"Thy kingdom come, Thy will be done" — Expresses surrender to God's will and desire for His reign of justice and peace on earth.

"Give us this day our daily bread" — A request for both material needs (food, shelter) and spiritual nourishment (especially the Eucharist).

"Forgive us our trespasses, as we forgive those who trespass against us" — Calls us to seek God's mercy while committing to extend forgiveness to others.

"Lead us not into temptation, but deliver us from evil" — Asks for protection from sin, the devil, and all forms of evil.

For Catholics, this prayer is not only recited in daily devotion but also forms a central part of the Mass, prayed together before receiving the Eucharist. It is both communal ("our Father") and deeply personal, teaching humility, dependence on God, and the call to live in charity with others.

Traditional Hoodoo Perspective

Within African American Hoodoo tradition, the Our Father is often prayed to align one's will with Divine will before beginning any working. It is a spiritual centering prayer — a way of ensuring that the power you call upon comes through the highest source and is directed for the greatest good. Praying it before spells, rootwork, or readings is common to "set the table" spiritually. The line "Give us this day our daily bread" is often understood not just as food, but as all provision —

money, opportunities, strength, and blessings — making it a prosperity invocation as well. "Deliver us from evil" can be seen as a protective working in itself, sending away malice, envy, and any spiritual crossings.

My Perspective

For me, the Our Father is a beautiful gift from Jesus, but it also comes with a call to deep self-awareness. Neville Goddard said the Father is within us — the Kingdom is within us — so if I am praying "Thy Kingdom come, Thy will be done," I am also inviting the world of my own mind and soul to manifest outward. That means my "Kingdom" must be clean.

If I am full of chaos, resentment, or doubt, then the "will" I am agreeing to might not be in perfect alignment with Divine truth. This prayer reminds me to keep my inner life pure so that what I manifest reflects God's wholeness. When I pray these words, I feel called to cleanse — not just my space, but my thoughts, emotions, and spirit.

I encourage you to use this prayer as a mirror for your inner condition. As you speak each line, feel it as a declaration of what is already true within you. Let it cleanse your soul. Let it bring to the surface anything that is out of alignment so that you can heal it. For deeper mental and spiritual cleansing, I often pray the St. Michael Chaplet, which I find clears my mind and heart so that when I pray Our Father, it comes from the deepest, truest place.

I also want to offer a word of discernment about how this prayer is used. In the film Sinners, there's a striking scene where the pastor's son prays the Our Father in front of a vampire, and the vampire prays right along with him. To me, this is a reminder that the Our Father is not solely a prayer of protection, nor is it automatically a weapon against evil like the St. Michael Prayer is. The words themselves speak about alignment, manifestation, and surrender to Divine will — not specifically exorcism or a "vampire deterrent". The protection you feel when praying it comes from the energy and authority you put into it. Without your spiritual force behind it, even the most sacred words can be repeated by those without holy intent.

Additional Note on Interpretation

Different traditions — and even individual teachers within those traditions — interpret this prayer in different ways. The Catholic Church, for example, has long taught that "Give us this day our daily bread" can refer to the Eucharist. I once saw a Catholic influencer on YouTube strongly promote that interpretation, linking it to the importance of the sacrament. While some agreed in the comments, others disagreed — and I personally find that interpretation to be both limiting and, in this case, a stretch. In the Hoodoo perspective, and in my own mystical reading, this phrase is about provision in all forms, not the Eucharist.

Of course, if the Eucharistic meaning resonates with you, you are free to hold that view — faith is deeply personal. But I also want to caution that people can sometimes bend a text to fit their preferred theology. Even this influencer's deep dive into the Greek (noting the repetition of "day") did not convince me otherwise. In Hoodoo, this line has always been about daily sustenance — physical, spiritual, emotional, and financial — and that is the understanding I offer here.

Hail Mary

Traditional Text

Hail Mary, full of grace, the Lord is with thee;

Blessed art thou amongst women,

And blessed is the fruit of thy womb, Jesus.

Holy Mary, Mother of God,

Pray for us sinners, now and at the hour of our death. Amen.

Traditional Catholic Perspective

The Hail Mary is one of the most iconic Catholic prayers, rooted directly in Scripture.

The first part — "Hail Mary, full of grace, the Lord is with thee" — comes from the Angel Gabriel's greeting at the Annunciation (Luke 1:28).

"Blessed art thou amongst women and blessed is the fruit of thy womb" is Elizabeth's greeting at the Visitation (Luke 1:42).

The second half — "Holy Mary, Mother of God, pray for us sinners now and at the hour of our death"— is a later addition from the Catholic Church, affirming Mary as Theotokos (God-bearer) and asking for her intercession.

For Catholics, it is both a praise of Mary's role in salvation and a petition for her aid throughout life and especially at death.

Traditional Hoodoo Perspective

In African American Hoodoo tradition, the Hail Mary is a powerful petition-prayer that carries the weight of Scripture and the energy of repetition. While Mary is respected as a mother figure and intercessor, the words themselves are also understood to activate blessing and favor when spoken with faith. Hoodoo practitioners may pray the Hail Mary:

- For protection (especially of children and the home)

- For blessings in fertility, childbirth, or creativity

- For favor and grace in a situation where divine influence is needed

The prayer is often integrated into working with candles, roots, or charms, but can also be spoken alone as a charm of spoken power.

My Perspective

The Hail Mary is one of my favorite prayers, and one of the most recognizable in the world — often associated with Catholicism, but not owned by it. I am not Catholic, yet I love this prayer because of my relationship with Mary. Even if you don't see Mary as a divine being, you can still pray this prayer by reframing her as many Christian mystics have: a representation of your divine imagination — as Neville Goddard described — or as a sacred aspect of your own being.

The first half of the prayer is straight from the Bible, but it also contains a blueprint for manifestation:

"Full of grace, the Lord is with thee" — reminding us that we, too, can live in a state of grace where divine presence is with us.

"Blessed art thou amongst women" — pointing to the elevated state that comes from accepting grace.

"Blessed is the fruit of thy womb" — showing that from this divine state comes the manifestation of something blessed and holy.

The latter half of the prayer once challenged me. I initially resisted "pray for us sinners now and at the hour of our death", because I didn't see myself as a sinner. But I came to understand this line differently — it's not just for me, it's for us. It's intercession for others as well, including those in their final moments of life. As someone who works as a psychopomp, this line became sacred to me. It's a way of standing with Mary for souls crossing over, even if I've never met them.

Holy Mary, Mother of God is a line I especially love as someone outside of traditional Christianity. It connects Mary to the archetype of the divine mother found in many cultures and affirms that women can birth gods — physically or metaphorically. Whether one accepts the theological implications or not, the mystical depth remains.

Additional Notes

Some interpret give us this day our daily bread in the Our Father as referring to the Eucharist; in the Hail Mary, similar theological debates arise over Mother of God. Interpretations vary, and not all will resonate.

The prayer is not only about intercession; it is also about embodying grace and creating from a divine state of being.

From a magical perspective, the Hail Mary can be used for manifestation, blessing, and protection — but the energy comes from the one praying as much as from the words themselves.

Glory Be

Traditional Text

Glory be to the Father, and to the Son, and to the Holy Spirit, As it was in the beginning, is now, and ever shall be, world without end. Amen.

Traditional Catholic Perspective

The Glory Be, also known as the Doxology, is a short prayer of praise to the Holy Trinity. In Catholic tradition, it affirms God's eternal nature — without beginning or end — and recognizes the Father, Son, and Holy Spirit as equally divine.

It's often prayed at the conclusion of each decade of the rosary, serving as a seal of praise that bookends the meditative mystery. For Catholics, it is a reminder that God's glory exists outside the limits of time and continues into eternity.

Traditional Hoodoo Perspective

In Hoodoo practice, especially where biblical prayers are integrated into spiritual work, the Glory Be is a compact yet potent invocation of divine power. Because it praises the fullness of God — past, present, and future — it can be used to "lock in" a petition, blessing, or protective working. It's the verbal equivalent of tying off a knot, fixing a charm, or sealing a prayer so its influence continues indefinitely.

The phrase world without end carries an energy of endurance and unbroken blessing, which in magical work can be applied to petitions for long-lasting results, generational protection, or ongoing spiritual favor.

My Perspective

I love the Glory Be. I often find myself praying it in Latin (Gloria Patri, et Filio, et Spiritui Sancto...) because the rhythm and sound feel so ancient and sacred. This prayer touches on profound spiritual laws — the reality that there is only the now, that time as we perceive it is an illusion, and that the divine presence is eternal.

When I say world without end, I feel deep comfort — especially in a world where we sometimes fear war, destruction, or global endings. This prayer reminds me that while worlds and empires may shift, divine creation itself is without end.

The line as it was in the beginning, is now, and ever shall be has a cosmic quality for me. It reminds me that the prayers I say now ripple across time. They reach into my past to heal and strengthen me, extend into my future to prepare and bless me, and touch others across time as well.

This is one of those prayers that carries a universal mystical truth found in many traditions: energy does not die, creation continues, and the eternal is always present.

Neville Goddard's teachings often come to mind here — that the Father, Son, and Holy Spirit are not distant figures, but aspects of our own consciousness:

- **The Father** as the origin or source — the "I AM" within us.

- **The Son** as the manifestation of that source — what we bring into form.

- **The Holy Spirit** as the movement of creation — the breath, inspiration, and power that animates change.

Even though this prayer is short, it's densely packed with mystical depth. You can repeat it many times and find new meaning in it each time, almost like a gemstone that refracts light differently when turned.

Additional Notes

The Glory Be can also be seen as a prayer of deep gratitude — giving glory to the Father, the Son, and the Holy Spirit throughout all time. In this way, it becomes a continuous offering of thanks for what has been, what is, and what is to come, aligning your spirit with a timeless flow of praise and appreciation.

Fatima Prayer

Traditional Text

O my Jesus, forgive us our sins, save us from the fires of hell,

Lead all souls to Heaven, especially those in most need of Thy mercy.

Traditional Catholic Perspective

The Fatima Prayer originated from the apparitions at Fatima, Portugal in 1917, where the Virgin Mary appeared to three shepherd children. According to the accounts, the children first received visits from an angel who taught them preparatory prayers before being given this prayer by Mary.

In Catholic tradition, this prayer is said after each decade of the rosary (though it is optional) as an act of penance and intercession. It asks for Christ's mercy not only on ourselves, but on all souls, with special emphasis on those most in need. The fires of hell are understood as eternal separation from God, and this prayer is a plea for universal salvation through Christ's mercy.

Traditional Hoodoo Perspective

Within a Hoodoo framework, the Fatima Prayer can be understood as a cleansing and intercessory work. Just as baths, floor washes, or smudges remove spiritual debris, this prayer "washes" the spirit with divine mercy. It resets spiritual alignment before stepping into deeper petition or magical work.

Because Hoodoo blends biblical faith with folk magic, the intercessory aspect — "especially those in most need of Thy mercy" — functions much like community or ancestor petitions. One is not simply working for oneself, but extending blessing to others, which in turn builds reciprocal spiritual goodwill. The language of being saved from "fires" also resonates with Hoodoo's focus on turning back harmful conditions — whether those fires are literal dangers, destructive emotions, or spiritual attacks.

My Perspective

At first, I didn't include the Fatima Prayer in my rosary because I knew it was optional, and I didn't yet feel a conscious connection to Jesus as a literal being. My relationship to Christ shifted when I began to see Jesus not as a figure from history alone, but as an energy — Christ Consciousness, the Christ within me — and also as a living manifestation of divine power. That deeper understanding opened my heart to this prayer, and now I truly love it.

I find it deeply moving that this prayer was given to the children at Fatima by the Virgin Mary herself. To me, that makes it an even more intimate and intentional gift — a prayer she personally placed into the world as a way for us to approach God's mercy. I see it as a spiritual cleansing, a "wash" of the soul that clears anything blocking grace from flowing. The phrase "forgive us our sins" feels like the gentle sweep of divine light preparing us to receive more fully.

The inclusiveness of "especially those in most need of Thy mercy" makes the Fatima Prayer feel incredibly alive for me because it elevates my rosary work beyond being prayers for myself alone. It becomes an offering for the world. After a day of not doing the rosary or any prayers, I had a dream in which I heard the voice of God and saw Archangel Michael and a part of their message within that striking dream was that: my rosary work matters because it sends prayers rippling out — across time, across locations, across lands — for others.

When I pray "O my Jesus, forgive us our sins"..., I'm not only inviting the activation of Christ within myself but calling for that divine spark to awaken within others. This is part of my soul work. I believe that when we are activated, our very energy changes, and the world around us shifts in response. Other people — without force, without manipulation — can be elevated simply by our presence and vibration.

This is why I reject the manipulative way I sometimes see prayer used by certain Catholic influencers, who pray for others to "convert" or abandon who they are in order to conform to a single religious mold. To me, that is prayer as a form of controlling witchcraft, not love. My intercessory prayer is not about changing someone into something else; it's about calling forth their truest, happiest, most aware self — whatever language or path they choose to describe that awakening.

In this way, the Fatima Prayer is not just a devotional add-on. It's a living reminder that my growth, my alignment, and my prayers are never just for me. They are meant to help create the conditions where others can awaken, too — and that, to me, is one of the most loving uses of prayer there is.

Additional Notes

This prayer can be used intentionally before any major spiritual working as a way to clear blockages and prepare the heart. Its intercessory nature also makes it effective for community-focused or ancestral work, especially when one seeks to lift others out of harmful states or open them to spiritual awakening.

6

What are the Rosary's Mysteries?

The rosary is a powerful prayer that leads you to reflect on the lives of Mary and Jesus through 20 Gospel mysteries. These are grouped into four categories: Joyful, Sorrowful, Glorious, and Luminous. Each set focuses on key moments in the Gospel, prayed on specific days to foster daily meditation.

Joyful Mysteries: Meditate on Christ's early life (prayed on Mondays and Saturdays).

1. The Annunciation
2. The Visitation
3. The Nativity
4. The Presentation in the Temple
5. The Finding of the Child Jesus in the Temple

Sorrowful Mysteries: Reflect on Christ's suffering and passion (prayed on Tuesdays and Fridays).

1. The Agony in the Garden
2. The Scourging at the Pillar
3. The Crowning with Thorns
4. The Carrying of the Cross
5. The Crucifixion and Death of Jesus

Glorious Mysteries: Celebrate Christ's victory over death and the glory of heaven (prayed on Wednesdays and Sundays).

1. The Resurrection
2. The Ascension
3. The Descent of the Holy Spirit
4. The Assumption of Mary
5. The Coronation of Mary as Queen of Heaven

Luminous Mysteries: Contemplate moments of Jesus' ministry and divine revelation (prayed on Thursdays).

1. The Baptism of Jesus in the Jordan
2. The Wedding at Cana
3. The Proclamation of the Kingdom of God
4. The Transfiguration
5. The Institution of the Eucharist

Beyond traditional Catholic devotion, the mysteries of the rosary hold deeper layers of meaning. They can be seen as cycles of transformation, spiritual lessons, and even tools for manifestation. Each decade becomes both a meditation and a spiritual act, drawing you closer to divine wisdom. For example:

- The **Seven Sorrows of Mary**, often prayed separately, teach surrender, resilience, and trust, mirroring the spiritual steps of manifestation.
- The **Assumption and Coronation of Mary** symbolize ascension into spiritual authority and fulfillment of purpose.
- The **Wedding at Cana** highlights abundance, offering a lesson in aligning actions with divine guidance to turn lack into overflow.

The Joyful Mysteries can inspire gratitude, blessings, and fresh beginnings. The Sorrowful Mysteries offer strength, protection, and perseverance. The Glorious Mysteries lead to elevation, victory, and divine partnership, while the Luminous Mysteries provide clarity, revelation, and alignment with purpose.

In traditions like the Hoodoo Rosary, these mysteries transcend their Catholic roots, transforming into living spiritual codes. They can be paired with Psalms, petitions, or offerings, making each bead not just a meditation but a magical act that moves you closer to your desires while deepening your spiritual journey.

But before you begin working the Hoodoo Rosary it is important that you have a general understanding of the rosary's mysteries.

What follows is a Hoodoo breakdown of all of the Rosary Mysteries, along with reflections to guide your prayers. I suggest taking a week to pray the mysteries following the Church's weekly calendar and using the information here as a reference during the process. You can also dedicate yourself to praying the 7 Joys of Mary or the 7 Sorrows of Mary, deepening your connection to her life and virtues. This will give you time to really get to know the prayers, the Bible stories within the rosary, the characters of the rosary, and your own rosary well so that you will be comfortable enough to work the Hoodoo Rosary. As you pray the traditional mysteries on your own, you'll start to uncover the mysteries for yourself—finding your own insights and noticing things that may not be explicitly detailed. Trust the process and let it guide you deeper.

7

The Joyful Mysteries

The Joyful Mysteries open the rosary with the tender and miraculous beginnings of the life of Jesus Christ and the unfolding mission of the Virgin Mary. Prayed on Mondays and Saturdays in Catholic tradition, these five sacred events carry the vibration of hope, promise, and divine fulfillment. They remind us that God often begins His greatest works in the quiet, unseen places—within wombs, within homes, within hearts—and calls us to recognize the miraculous even in the ordinary.

Each mystery reveals a step in the spiritual path of creation: receiving divine vision, embracing the call, nurturing the seed of promise, and bearing it forth into the world. These are mysteries of becoming—of saying "yes" to what Heaven plants within you, even when you do not see the fullness of the outcome.

From a Hoodoo perspective, the Joyful Mysteries are mysteries of manifestation magic and ancestral blessing. They hold deep roots in the work of calling in, blessing the home, nurturing the seed, safe delivery, and dedicating a life to divine service. They are mysteries of invitation—welcoming not just the Christ Child, but also the gifts, opportunities, and spiritual helpers Heaven sends to you.

When prayed with intention, the Joyful Mysteries are powerful for:

- Drawing in blessings and new beginnings.
- Increasing fertility—of the body, mind, and spirit.
- Gaining the courage to step into your calling.
- Protecting what is newly birthed from harm or misfortune.
- Deepening your bond with your ancestors, guides, and the Divine Mother.

As you pray through these mysteries, imagine each bead as a seed you plant in the rich soil of your life. Your words are the water. Your faith is the sunlight. And in time, Heaven will grow what you have sown.

In the sections that follow, we will walk through each Joyful Mystery with:

- The scriptural account of the event.
- Spiritual meanings and mystical layers.
- Keys for unlocking the power of each mystery in your life.
- Practical affirmations to carry the truth of each meditation into your daily walk.

The Annunciation

In the sixth month of Elizabeth's pregnancy, God sent the angel Gabriel to Nazareth, a town in Galilee, to a virgin pledged to be married to a man named Joseph, a descendant of David. The virgin's name was Mary. The angel went to her and said, "Greetings, you who are highly favored! The Lord is with you."

Mary was greatly troubled at his words and wondered what kind of greeting this might be. But the angel said to her, "Do not be afraid, Mary; you have found favor with God. You will conceive and give birth to a son, and you are to call him Jesus. He will be great and will be called the Son of the Most High. The Lord God will give him the throne of his father David, and he will reign over Jacob's descendants forever; his kingdom will never end."

"How will this be," Mary asked the angel, "since I am a virgin?"

The angel answered, "The Holy Spirit will come on you, and the power of the Most High will overshadow you. So the holy one to be born will be called the Son of God. Even Elizabeth your relative is going to have a child in her old age, and she who was said to be unable to conceive is in her sixth month. For no word from God will ever fail."

"I am the Lord's servant," Mary answered. "May your word to me be fulfilled." Then the angel left her.
— Luke 1:26–38

Spiritual Meaning

The Annunciation is the moment when the divine interrupts the ordinary with a holy invitation. Mary, going about her day, receives an unexpected message from Gabriel that will change her life and the course of history.

It teaches us to stay ready so you don't have to get ready — divine opportunities can come when we least expect them. The Annunciation also honors the role of informed consent in spiritual calling. Mary did not immediately say yes; she asked a question — "How will this be?" — seeking understanding before giving her consent. This is a powerful reminder that saying yes to God doesn't mean abandoning wisdom or self-agency.

Mystically, the Annunciation is about saying yes to the mystery of God, even when it disrupts our plans. Mary had plans to marry Joseph; her "yes" risked misunderstanding, judgment, and even danger. Yet she embraced the unknown because she trusted the divine purpose.

Hoodoo Insights

In Hoodoo, the Annunciation reflects the moment a calling, vision, or opportunity is "spoken into" your life. Words are power, and a divine message is like a spiritual seed planted within you. Just as Mary conceived when the Holy Spirit came upon her, a conjure worker knows that once a word of blessing is spoken over you, it begins to manifest in the unseen.

The emphasis on readiness also echoes conjure principles: keep your spiritual house in order so that when opportunity arrives, you are in a position to receive it without delay.

Keys for Prayer & Manifestation

Be Ready for the Divine: Maintain spiritual readiness for sudden blessings or assignments.

Ask for Clarity: Informed consent is part of a healthy spiritual relationship.

Say Yes to the Unknown: Trust that divine disruption can lead to divine destiny.

Honor the Power of the Word: Spoken blessings have creative force.

Align Your Life: Keep your inner and outer life in order so you can receive fully.

Affirmations

"I am ready for divine opportunities."

"My consent is sacred, and I give it freely to what serves my highest good."

"I welcome the mysteries of God into my life."

"Even in uncertainty, I trust Spirit's plan for me."

The Visitation

At that time Mary got ready and hurried to a town in the hill country of Judea, where she entered Zechariah's home and greeted Elizabeth. When Elizabeth heard Mary's greeting, the baby leaped in her womb, and Elizabeth was filled with the Holy Spirit. In a loud voice she exclaimed: "Blessed are you among women, and blessed is the child you will bear! But why am I so favored, that the mother of my Lord should come to me? As soon as the sound of your greeting reached my ears, the baby in my womb leaped for joy. Blessed is she who has believed that the Lord would fulfill his promises to her!" — **Luke 1:39-45**

Spiritual Meaning

The Visitation is a celebration of divine connection — a meeting of souls who recognize each other's sacred calling. It is about the bonds of family, both by blood and by spirit, and about the mutual strengthening that occurs when two people walking parallel divine paths come together.

Mary's visit to Elizabeth also shows her humility and tenderness. Though she had just received the greatest news in history, she did not isolate herself or focus solely on her own situation; she made the long journey to be with someone she trusted and loved. This is the spirit of sacred sisterhood — the knowing that in times of great change or great joy, we need the support and encouragement of those who understand us.

Hoodoo Insights

From a Hoodoo perspective, the Visitation speaks to the recognition of divine power in others — real recognizes real. When Elizabeth heard Mary's greeting, her spirit recognized the Christ within Mary, and John leapt in her womb in confirmation. In our own lives, we often meet people whose presence awakens something deep in us, as if our souls are saying, Yes, I know you. I know what you carry.

The Visitation also teaches the grace of celebrating another's blessings without jealousy. Elizabeth, though she was older and carrying a miraculous child herself, allowed herself to be moved by the Holy Spirit to bless Mary wholeheartedly. She offered genuine praise without comparison or competition. This is a sacred art in itself — to rejoice in another's divine calling as if it were your own.

The Magnificat that follows is Mary's song of praise to God, a declaration of divine justice, mercy, and reversal of fortune. It is a reminder that in the midst of shared joy, we should lift our voices to give thanks and acknowledge the One from whom all blessings flow.

Keys for Prayer and Manifestation

Sisterhood & Family Bonds: The Visitation calls us to cherish the trusted people who walk with us in seasons of change, joy, and uncertainty.

Recognition of the Divine in Others: Just as John recognized Christ from the womb, we can train our hearts to recognize those carrying divine purpose.

Humility in Service: Even when entrusted with something great, choose to serve, visit, and encourage others.

Celebration Without Envy: Bless others' victories freely, knowing that divine blessings multiply in an atmosphere of mutual joy.

Praise as Power: Let gratitude and praise seal moments of shared joy, as Mary did with the Magnificat.

Affirmations

I am surrounded by those who see and celebrate the divine within me.

I recognize and rejoice in the blessings of others.

My soul leaps in the presence of true spiritual kinship.

I speak blessings over those who walk in divine purpose.

My relationships are filled with holy trust, joy, and support.

The Nativity

and she gave birth to her firstborn, a son. She wrapped him in cloths and placed him in a manger, because there was no guest room available for them.

And there were shepherds living out in the fields nearby, keeping watch over their flocks at night. An angel of the Lord appeared to them, and the glory of the Lord shone around them, and they were terrified. But the angel said to them, "Do not be afraid. I bring you good news that will cause great joy for all the people. Today in the town of David a Savior has been born to you; he is the Messiah, the Lord. — **Luke 2:7–11**

Spiritual Meaning

The Nativity shows us that God's plan may not unfold in the way we imagined — but it will always provide what is necessary. Mary may have dreamed of a comfortable, prepared space to give birth, but instead found herself in a stable, laying her child in a manger. Even so, she had shelter, she had Joseph, and she had the strength to bring forth life.

It is a reminder that divine purpose often arrives in humble circumstances, and that beauty and holiness are not dependent on wealth, status, or comfort. The presence of animals, the earthy smell of hay, the simplicity of the setting — all point to the truth that we are human and divine, spirit and flesh, and deeply connected to creation.

Mystically, the Nativity speaks to the importance of guarding what we birth. When we swaddle a newborn, we keep them safe, warm, and close — we don't immediately expose them to the world. Likewise, when we birth something new — a vision, a calling, a spiritual gift — it must be nurtured and protected before it is shared widely. Mary knew her role as protector as well as mother, safeguarding this holy child until the appointed time.

Hoodoo Insights

In the Hoodoo tradition, The Nativity resonates with the principle of spiritual incubation — keeping new blessings covered and protected until they are strong enough to withstand the world. Just as Mary swaddled Jesus, rootworkers often "wrap" their work — in cloth, jars, or hidden places — so it can grow in strength before it is revealed.

The humble birth setting also reminds conjure practitioners that the most powerful workings can be done with the simplest of materials. Spirit is not impressed by luxury — it responds to sincerity, faith, and intention.

Keys for Prayer & Manifestation

Trust the Provision: Even if things don't go as planned, you will have what you truly need.

Value Humble Beginnings: Great blessings can come from the simplest places.

Honor Your Humanity: Embrace the connection to all living beings, including the animal world.

Guard the New: Protect what you are birthing spiritually until it is ready for the world.

See Beauty in Simplicity: Recognize holiness in the everyday and the ordinary.

Affirmations

I trust that I will always have what I need, even if it arrives in unexpected ways.

My humble beginnings are the soil for great blessings.

I honor and protect what I birth spiritually and physically.

I am connected to all creation, human and animal alike.

I find holiness in simplicity and gratitude in provision.

The Presentation in the Temple

"When the time came for the purification rites required by the Law of Moses, Joseph and Mary took him to Jerusalem to present him to the Lord (as it is written in the Law of the Lord, 'Every firstborn male is to be consecrated to the Lord'), and to offer a sacrifice in keeping with what is said in the Law of the Lord: 'a pair of doves or two young pigeons.' Now there was a man in Jerusalem called Simeon, who was righteous and devout. He was waiting for the consolation of Israel, and the Holy Spirit was on him. It had been revealed to him by the Holy Spirit that he would not die before he had seen the Lord's Messiah.Moved by the Spirit, he went into the temple courts. When the parents brought in the child Jesus to do for him what the custom of the Law required, Simeon took him in his arms and praised God, saying: 'Sovereign Lord, as you have promised, you may now dismiss your servant in peace.

For my eyes have seen your salvation, which you have prepared in the sight of all nations: a light for revelation to the Gentiles, and the glory of your people Israel.' The child's father and mother marveled at what was said about him." — **Luke 2:22-33**

Spiritual Meaning

The Presentation in the Temple reminds us that even in our divinity, we live in a world of structures, traditions, and laws — and there is wisdom in honoring them when they are aligned with truth. Jesus, Mary, and Joseph were pure and chosen, yet they still fulfilled the requirements of their faith, presenting Jesus at the temple and offering the humble sacrifice of two doves.

It also teaches discernment in prophecy. Mary and Joseph listened to Simeon — a man they did not know — yet they recognized the Spirit's truth in his words. They did not dismiss the prophecy because of its unexpected source, nor did they blindly accept it without spiritual resonance. They marveled because it confirmed what they already knew deep within.

The Presentation also reveals the beauty of public blessing. This moment was not hidden in secrecy; it was a shared recognition of Jesus' mission. And yet, in the midst of that public blessing, Mary is also given a private prophecy — that a sword will pierce her own soul. The sacred path often holds both glory and sorrow in the same breath.

Hoodoo Insights

In Hoodoo, this mystery reflects the act of dedicating — bringing a child, object, or work to be blessed and set apart for divine purpose. It mirrors the practice of taking something new into sacred space so it is not merely yours, but God's.

The discernment Mary and Joseph show in receiving prophecy also aligns with conjure wisdom: not every message is for you, and not every voice is anointed. But when the Spirit speaks through someone, you will know. This is why we "test the spirit" and trust the inner witness.

Keys for Prayer & Manifestation

Honor Sacred Traditions: Even the divine honors the rhythm of holy customs.

Dedicate Your Work: Bless what you birth before sending it into the world.

Discern the Source: Receive only what resonates with Spirit and truth.

Hold Both Joy and Sorrow: Prophecy may prepare you for glory and hardship together.

Invite Public Blessing: Allow others to witness and affirm your divine calling.

Affirmations

I honor sacred traditions that keep me aligned with the divine.

I dedicate my works, gifts, and creations to God.

I trust my spirit to discern which messages are true.

I accept both joy and challenge as part of my sacred path.

I welcome blessings from those the Spirit sends into my life.

The Finding in the Temple

"Every year Jesus' parents went to Jerusalem for the Festival of the Passover. When he was twelve years old, they went up to the festival, according to the custom. After the festival was over, while his parents were returning home, the boy Jesus stayed behind in Jerusalem, but they were unaware of it. Thinking he was in their company, they traveled on for a day. Then they began looking for him among their relatives and friends. When they did not find him, they went back to Jerusalem to look for him. After three days they found him in the temple courts, sitting among the teachers, listening to them and asking them questions. Everyone who heard him was amazed at his understanding and his answers. When his parents saw him, they were astonished. His mother said to him, 'Son, why have you treated us like this? Your father and I have been anxiously searching for you.' 'Why were you searching for me?' he asked. 'Didn't you know I had to be in my Father's house?' But they did not understand what he was saying to them." — **Luke 2:41-50**

Spiritual Meaning

The Finding in the Temple reflects the spiritual journey each of us undertakes — including moments when we feel we have "lost" God. This can be a dark night of the soul: we search anxiously, wondering why the presence of the divine feels so far away.

Yet, as this mystery shows, God is never truly lost to us. Jesus was not far; He was in the place He was meant to be. Sometimes the divine is found right where tradition has preserved it — in the temple, in sacred community, in the expected places we may overlook in our search for something extraordinary.

It also teaches holy boldness. Even as a young boy surrounded by elders, Jesus asked questions and engaged in deep conversation. He did not wait for permission or a title to speak and to learn. This is a reminder that spiritual wisdom is not bound by age or rank — the Spirit moves where it will.

Hoodoo Insights

In Hoodoo, "finding in the temple" parallels the process of reconnecting with your altar or your root. Sometimes life pulls you away from consistent prayer or ritual, and there's a moment when you "find" your practice again — and it feels like coming home.

The three days Mary and Joseph searched echo the pattern of spiritual trial and resurrection. Three days is the time it takes for transformation to begin: a spiritual search followed by renewal. This is a mystery about persistence — if you keep looking, you will find what was lost.

Keys for Prayer & Manifestation

Accept the Search: Losing sight of the divine can be part of the journey.

Look in Both New and Old Places: The sacred can be found in tradition as much as in novelty.

Ask Questions Boldly: Do not let age, title, or status silence your curiosity.

Recognize God's Nearness: The divine is often closer than we think.

Trust the Pattern of Return: A loss can lead to a deeper reconnection.

Affirmations

I trust that even when I feel lost, God is near.

I allow myself to find the sacred in both ancient and new places.

I ask questions with courage and curiosity.

I honor my spiritual searches as part of my growth.

I welcome reconnection with the divine in its perfect time.

8

The Sorrowful Mysteries

The Sorrowful Mysteries invite us to walk with Jesus through the most agonizing hours of His earthly life — moments of betrayal, injustice, physical suffering, and death. They are not easy to meditate on, yet they are deeply transformative. They remind us that suffering is not without meaning, that even in the darkest night, divine purpose can shine through.

Where the Joyful Mysteries teach us to say yes to God and rejoice in His promises, the Sorrowful Mysteries teach us to hold fast when saying yes leads to trials. They take us into the heart of sacrifice, courage, and unwavering love.

In Catholic devotion, these mysteries are traditionally prayed on Tuesdays and Fridays, and daily during the season of Lent. But in a mystical and Hoodoo perspective, they are powerful any time you need strength, endurance, protection, or liberation from bondage — both spiritual and earthly.

Each Sorrowful Mystery is more than a retelling of events; it is a key to understanding the universal experience of human suffering. They show us that pain can be a gateway to transformation, that endurance can deepen wisdom, and that love — real love — is always willing to bear the weight of another.

Why These Mysteries Matter Now

For the mystic, the Sorrowful Mysteries are not merely about remembering the past. They are living spiritual tools for navigating betrayal, injustice, spiritual warfare, and personal trials today.

In Hoodoo and other African American spiritual traditions, prayers born out of suffering carry a special kind of power — the power of endurance that transforms. The Sorrowful Mysteries mirror the spiritual songs sung by enslaved people, the prayers whispered by the oppressed, and the endurance of those who stand their ground against forces meant to break them.

They also speak to our own inner battles:

- The Gethsemane moments when we must choose obedience over comfort.

- The scourging moments when the world strips away our dignity.

- The crowning moments when we are mocked for who we are or what we believe.

- The carrying moments when we bear burdens not entirely our own.

- The crucifixion moments when something must die so something greater can live.

Praying the Sorrowful Mysteries

As you enter into these meditations, invite Mary — the one who walked each step beside her Son — to walk with you. Her intercession and her maternal heart are a shield in the midst of sorrow.

You may notice that praying these mysteries can bring to the surface your own wounds, your own betrayals, and your own moments of despair. This is not to overwhelm you, but to let grace touch those places. Just as the Passion of Christ transformed the cross from a symbol of shame into a symbol of victory, so too can your sorrows be transformed into a source of strength and blessing.

In the sections that follow, we will walk through each Sorrowful Mystery with:

- The scriptural account of the event.

- Spiritual meanings and mystical layers.

- Keys for unlocking the power of each mystery in your life.

- Practical affirmations to carry the truth of each meditation into your daily walk.

The Scourging

> Then Pilate took Jesus and had him flogged. — **John 19:1**

Spiritual Meaning

The Scourging at the Pillar is one of the most visceral, physical moments of the Passion. Jesus, innocent and pure, is brutally beaten — not for guilt, but because the world, in its fear and corruption, lashes out at what it cannot control.

Spiritually, this mystery invites us into the reality that living in truth sometimes means enduring the blows of misunderstanding, betrayal, and injustice. It is a reminder that righteousness does not shield us from pain; rather, it calls us to endure it with dignity.

And here's an important truth — spirituality does not grant us a pass from physical suffering. Some believe that deep prayer, magic, or enlightenment will let them sidestep pain entirely. But the scourging shows us otherwise: sometimes we must fully experience the body's trials, be present in the discomfort, and move through the rawness of the human condition. There is magic in the physical — but it is not always soft, fragrant, and beautiful. Sometimes the magic is gritty, aching, and unpolished, yet no less divine.

Hoodoo Insights

From a Hoodoo perspective, this is the part of the work where the cleansing is rough — where the uncrossing or reversal cuts deep. Sometimes, spiritual cleansing is not gentle. A bitter herb bath stings, a powerful crossing removal can shake up your life, and the results of a break-through working can look like chaos before they look like freedom.

The scourging also mirrors the idea of "taking the beating for the cause" — when we endure hardship, insults, or losses because of the truth we stand for. It teaches us that pain can be alchemical, turning shame into power and injustice into testimony.

Keys for Prayer and Manifestation

Stand Firm in Truth: Even when the blows come, do not abandon who you are.

Transform Pain into Power: Let trials refine you rather than define you.

See Attacks for What They Are: Often, hostility toward you reflects wounds in the attacker.

Endure with Purpose: Pain is not always meaningless — it can be the soil for future strength.

Remember the Cleansing Fire: The sting can be part of the purifying process.

Affirmations

No blow can take away my worth.

I am cleansed and strengthened through trial.

I endure with dignity and divine purpose.

I transform pain into testimony.

I am not defined by what has been done to me, but by who I choose to be.

The Agony in the Garden

Jesus went out as usual to the Mount of Olives, and his disciples followed him. On reaching the place, he said to them, "Pray that you will not fall into temptation." He withdrew about a stone's throw beyond them, knelt down and prayed, "Father, if you are willing, take this cup from me; yet not my will, but yours be done." An angel from heaven appeared to him and strengthened him. And being in anguish, he prayed more earnestly, and his sweat was like drops of blood falling to the ground.

When he rose from prayer and went back to the disciples, he found them asleep, exhausted from sorrow. "Why are you sleeping?" he asked them. "Get up and pray so that you will not fall into temptation." — **Luke 22:39–46**

Spiritual Meaning

The Agony in the Garden is the clearest reminder that prayer is not a guarantee that our will is done — it is an opening to Divine Will.

Here, Jesus — fully divine and fully human — asks for the cup to pass from Him. He voices a deep desire, yet He still yields to "not my will, but Yours be done."

This shows us that we can want things and pray for them with all sincerity, but it doesn't mean they will happen in the way we envision. Prayer is not the same as witchcraft in the sense of bending reality solely to our will. Instead, it's a conversation with God that says, If this aligns with the Divine, let it be so; if not, give me the peace, strength, and courage to walk through what comes.

If even Jesus, the Son of God, did not avoid a painful and unjust trial through prayer, then there must be something deeper in the human condition — something sacred and purposeful — in enduring certain trials. The Agony in the Garden reminds us that some things are not meant to be escaped, but transformed through our faith. His agony led to the Resurrection story, and so can ours.

Hoodoo Insights

Mystically, the Garden of Gethsemane is the inner chamber of the soul, the "night garden" where our will meets the Divine Will. It is the place where spiritual maturity blooms — not in getting what we want, but in choosing trust when the answer is no.

From a Hoodoo perspective, this moment is like the pause before a major working is completed. You've already set your intention, but there's a testing point — a threshold where doubt and fear rise. Just as we prepare spiritually before battle, Jesus prayed before entering His Passion, knowing that power without alignment can become destruction.

In conjure, we also recognize that not every door is meant to open, no matter how many prayers, psalms, or rituals we throw at it. Sometimes the "no" is the protection. Sometimes the hard road is the spell.

Keys for Prayer and Manifestation

Pray for Alignment, Not Control: True prayer seeks harmony with Divine Will.

Accept the Sacred "No": When God closes a path, it may be leading you to resurrection.

Prepare Before Trial: Just as Jesus prayed before His arrest, spiritually ready yourself before hardships.

Seek Strength, Not Escape: Ask for peace and courage more than you ask for the burden to vanish.

Remember the Bigger Story: The agony is not the end — it is a chapter before glory.

Affirmations

I trust the Divine even when the answer is no.

My prayers are an offering of alignment, not control.

Strength and peace are mine in every trial.

The hard path can still lead to resurrection.

Every "no" carries the seed of a greater "yes."

Crowning with Thorns

Then the soldiers of the governor took Jesus into the governor's headquarters, and they gathered the whole cohort around him. They stripped him and put a scarlet robe on him, and after twisting some thorns into a crown, they put it on his head. They put a reed in his right hand and knelt before him and mocked him, saying, "Hail, King of the Jews!" — **Matthew 27:27–29**

Spiritual Meaning

The Crowning with Thorns is a moment of sharp humiliation — both literally and figuratively. Jesus' true kingship is met with cruelty, sarcasm, and mockery. This mystery reveals the pain of being misunderstood, of standing in your truth while surrounded by those who not only fail to see it but actively degrade it.

It is a lesson in spiritual endurance: sometimes, walking your path means enduring the scorn of those who do not "get it." When you know who you are, you may attract ridicule from those threatened by your authenticity. They may twist your truth into a joke, taunt you for your light, or accuse you of arrogance — "Oh, you think you're too good for us." The walk of authenticity can be a lonely one, yet the crown — even when made of thorns — remains a crown.

Hoodoo Insights

In a Hoodoo framework, this is the spiritual test of standing in your power without flinching. In workings, it may be likened to the stage where you've claimed your blessing or title, and suddenly, spiritual resistance flares up. The "mockery" comes in many forms: gossip, disrespect, or tests to see if you will shrink back. Just as you wouldn't take off your crown to appease a heckler, you cannot set aside your anointing to avoid discomfort.

Keys for Prayer and Manifestation

Know Who You Are: Your worth does not decrease because others refuse to see it.

Wear the Crown Anyway: The crown may prick, but it still signifies your divine calling.

Endure Mockery with Grace: Their ridicule says more about their fear than about your truth.

Don't Shrink: Maintain your spiritual posture even in hostile environments.

Turn the Pain into Clarity: Every thorn can sharpen your awareness.

Affirmations

I wear my crown with courage, no matter the cost.

I am unshaken by the mockery of those who do not see me.

My worth is not determined by others' opinions.

I stand in my truth with dignity and power.

Every thorn strengthens my resolve.

The Carrying of the Cross

So they took Jesus; and carrying the cross by himself, he went out to what is called The Place of the Skull, which in Hebrew is called Golgotha. — **John 19:16–17**

Spiritual Meaning

The Carrying of the Cross is a raw, unfiltered image of personal responsibility. Jesus bears the very instrument of His own execution, step by agonizing step. No one else could take on His role; no one else could carry His mission to completion.

This mystery reminds us that, ultimately, your cross is yours to carry. It's not your friends, family, or even your spiritual allies who will bear it for you. Others may support or encourage you — as Simon of Cyrene helped Jesus for part of the way — but the essential weight is yours. Carrying the cross is a call to deep ownership of your life's mission, even when it's exhausting, isolating, or frightening.

To walk this path is to accept that if you truly know your calling, you must be willing to give everything for it — even your life as you know it.

Hoodoo Insights

In the Hoodoo tradition, this stage mirrors the work of carrying your own "load" in life — the spiritual obligations, oaths, or callings that no one else can fulfill for you. It's the gritty, lived reality of walking in your power.

Keys for Prayer and Manifestation

Own Your Path: Only you can fulfill your purpose.

Accept the Weight: Great callings carry great burdens.

Balance Spirit and Flesh: Honor your divine mission without denying your humanity.

Find Grace in the Strain: Every step with the cross is a step toward your fulfillment.

Receive Help Wisely: Accept support without relinquishing responsibility.

Affirmations

I embrace the weight of my calling with courage and strength.

I walk the intersection of divine and human with balance and grace.

My cross is mine, and I carry it with dignity.

I honor both my spiritual purpose and my human needs.

Every step I take brings me closer to divine fulfillment.

The Crucifixion and Death of Jesus

It was now about noon, and darkness came over the whole land until three in the afternoon, while the sun's light failed; and the curtain of the temple was torn in two. Then Jesus, crying with a loud voice, said, "Father, into your hands I commend my spirit." Having said this, he breathed his last.— **Luke 23:44–46**

Spiritual Meaning

The Crucifixion is often seen as the climax of suffering in the life of Jesus — a moment of agony, injustice, and apparent defeat. Yet, it is also a moment of profound union between the Son and the Father. In the act of dying, Jesus surrenders completely, trusting that His spirit will return to God.

The Crucifixion isn't merely about tragedy. It's about necessary transformation. For the Resurrection to happen, there must first be a death — the end of a chapter, a closing of a cycle. This death is not meaningless; it is the threshold between the story's deepest valley and its triumphant summit.

The Crucifixion reminds us that sometimes in life, something must end completely for something greater to be born. And often, the end doesn't erase the beauty or the love — it sanctifies it.

Hoodoo Insights

Mystically, the Crucifixion represents the ultimate surrender to divine timing and divine will. It's not an accident or a detour; it is a portal. Just as in spellwork or rootwork, sometimes a thing must be destroyed, cut away, or allowed to die before the desired manifestation can take shape.

The nails pinning Jesus to the cross are symbolic of being bound to your mission until it's fulfilled — even if it costs you everything. In Hoodoo, "crossing" has both a literal and a spiritual meaning, and here it represents crossing over from one state of being to another. The Crucifixion is that liminal space where endings and beginnings overlap.

Keys for Prayer and Manifestation

Honor Necessary Endings: Let go fully so the new can emerge.

Embrace Surrender: Give yourself entirely to divine alignment.

Find the Union in Loss: Even endings can hold deep connection to Spirit.

Accept the Story Arc: Every victory needs a turning point of sacrifice.

See Death as Transition: Not an end, but a doorway.

Affirmations

I release what must end so that resurrection can come.

I surrender to the divine plan with trust and openness.

Even in endings, I am held in God's embrace.

My sacrifices create space for transformation.

Death is never the end — it is the beginning of a greater chapter.

9

The Glorious Mysteries

The Glorious Mysteries invite us to step into the light after the shadows. If the Sorrowful Mysteries lead us into the depths of surrender, loss, and trial, the Glorious Mysteries call us to rise again — to see that beyond every death, there is life, and beyond every night, there is dawn.

These mysteries are not only about Christ's victory over death but also about our own transformation. They teach us that divine life is not meant to be trapped in a tomb; it is meant to be resurrected, glorified, and shared. In these meditations, we witness the movements of heaven breaking into earth: Christ rising, ascending, sending the Holy Spirit, and preparing a place for us in the eternal home.

These mysteries also carry a deeply mystical and practical truth:

- Resurrection doesn't always mean you come back in the same form — it means you come back changed.

- Ascension is the natural next step after resurrection — a lifting into a higher way of being.

- The coming of the Holy Spirit shows that divine presence is not limited to one person or place; it is poured out freely on all who are open to receive it.

- The Assumption of Mary reveals that the human and divine can unite so completely that even the body is welcomed into glory.

- The Coronation reminds us of our own inheritance as children of the divine — crowned with dignity, worth, and purpose.

In Hoodoo, these mysteries align with the power of rising after hardship, the sealing of spiritual work, and the crowning of success after long preparation. Just as in ritual, there is a rhythm: work, release, rise, and reign.

In the sections that follow, we will walk through each Glorious Mystery with:

- The scriptural account of the event.

- Spiritual meanings and mystical layers.

- Keys for unlocking the power of each mystery in your life.

- Practical affirmations to carry the truth of each meditation into your daily walk.

Resurrection

> But the angel said to the women, "Do not be afraid, for I know that you are looking for Jesus, who was crucified. He is not here; He has risen, just as He said. Come and see the place where He lay. Then go quickly and tell His disciples: 'He has risen from the dead and is going ahead of you into Galilee. There you will see Him.' Now I have told you." — **Matthew 28:5-7**

Spiritual Meaning

The Resurrection is the cornerstone of the Christian faith, the moment that proves death does not have the final word. It's not simply about Jesus coming back to life — it's about transformation into a higher form of life, one that is no longer bound by human limitations.

Mystically, the Resurrection affirms that every ending in our lives has the potential to be followed by a beginning that is greater than what came before. The grave is not the end of the story — it is the threshold into glory.

In addition one of the most striking things about the Resurrection is who was there to witness it. None of the prophets or great male religious figures were at the scene. Instead, it was an angel and the women

— those who loved Jesus deeply, stayed through the pain of the Crucifixion, and came in devotion to anoint His body.

There's a message here: divine revelation often comes first to those who show up in faithfulness, not necessarily to those with titles or public recognition. The women came to serve, to love, and to honor — and they became the first witnesses and messengers of the greatest miracle in history.

Hoodoo Insights

Power often moves in hidden channels. Sometimes, those on the margins — those without the "official" credentials — are the very ones entrusted with the deepest truths. The Resurrection reminds us to stay faithful to our work, even when it seems small or unnoticed, because heaven's announcements are often made to the quiet, devoted hearts.

Keys for Prayer and Manifestation

For New Life: Pray this mystery when you need a breakthrough after a long period of stagnation or hardship.

For Reversal of Loss: Use it as a spiritual petition for situations that seem "dead" but need revival — relationships, finances, health, or creative projects.

For Faithful Recognition: Call on this mystery to remind yourself that your devotion and daily acts of love position you for divine revelation.

For Hidden Workers: Ask God to honor the work you've done in secret, trusting that what's done in faith will bear public fruit in its time.

Affirmations

I rise with Christ into a higher form of life.

I am faithful in the hidden places, and heaven honors my devotion.

Every ending is a doorway to a greater beginning.

Revelation comes to me because I show up in love.

The Ascension

After He said this, He was taken up before their very eyes, and a cloud hid Him from their sight. They were looking intently up into the sky as He was going, when suddenly two men dressed in white stood beside them. "Men of Galilee," they said, "why do you stand here looking into the sky? This same Jesus, who has been taken from you into heaven, will come back in the same way you have seen Him go into heaven." — **Acts 1:9–11**

Spiritual Meaning

The Ascension is not a farewell — it's a transformation. Jesus' physical departure is the opening for a presence that is now everywhere, unhindered by time or space. His going up is a sign that the divine cannot be contained in one location.

This mystery tells us that some departures are not the end, but the beginning of a new kind of intimacy with the Divine. What appears as absence can be the birth of an even greater connection.

In addition, when the angels say that Jesus will return "in the same way you have seen Him go," it is a mystical clue. He went up to the Father — and this is where you will find Him too.

To "go up to the Father" is not to physically ascend into the clouds, but to enter that higher spiritual consciousness where the Father dwells. Jesus is within you, and when you rise into that inner communion with the Divine, you meet Him there.

This is not about looking outward to the sky for a distant return — it's about looking inward and upward in consciousness, finding that He has never truly left.

Hoodoo Insights

In Hoodoo, the Ascension can be seen as a rising above the weight of the world — a lifting of the spirit out of bondage and heaviness into freedom and higher power. Just as Jesus rose from the earth into the heavens, the practitioner calls on this mystery when seeking to rise above crosses, conditions, and enemies.

Keys for Prayer and Manifestation

For Divine Union: Pray this mystery to deepen your awareness that the Divine dwells within you.

For Spiritual Elevation: Ask for the ability to "rise" above lower states of fear, anger, or despair to meet God in a higher place.

For Inner Vision: Use the Ascension as a meditation on lifting your sight inward to see the Christ-light within.

For Faith in Cycles: This mystery reassures you that what departs will also return, transformed.

Affirmations

Jesus is within me; I find Him when I rise to the Father in spirit.

I lift my heart to the higher places where the Divine dwells.

I meet Christ in the sanctuary of my soul.

I trust that all that leaves returns in divine timing and form.

The Descent of the Holy Spirit

When the day of Pentecost came, they were all together in one place. Suddenly a sound like the blowing of a violent wind came from heaven and filled the whole house where they were sitting. They saw what seemed to be tongues of fire that separated and came to rest on each of them. All of them were filled with the Holy Spirit and began to speak in other tongues as the Spirit enabled them. Some, however, made fun of them and said, "They have had too much wine." — **Acts 2:1–4, 13**

Spiritual Meaning

The Descent of the Holy Spirit is the great ignition of divine fire within the disciples — the moment the promise of Christ becomes a living reality in their hearts. It is the ultimate empowerment, where heaven and earth meet in flame, and the Spirit's presence turns ordinary people into bold witnesses.

Yet, this miracle also reveals a sobering truth: not everyone will recognize the holy when it happens before their eyes. Some who saw the disciples filled with the Spirit thought they were drunk. This shows how spiritual realities can be misunderstood by those who are not attuned to them. What is sacred and transformative to you may appear as chaos, nonsense, or even foolishness to others. It's a reminder that you may operate on a wavelength so high and foreign that those who have never experienced divine fire will mislabel it.

This mystery calls us to remain faithful to our divine experience, regardless of how others interpret it. The Spirit's work in you is not for the approval of the crowd, but for the transformation of your soul and the manifestation of God's kingdom through your life.

Hoodoo Insights

In Hoodoo, the Descent of the Holy Spirit can be understood as the coming down of spiritual fire — power that anoints, inspires, and strengthens the worker. Just as the apostles received tongues of flame and boldness to go out and heal, teach, and cast out spirits, so too does the Holy Spirit empower the rootworker to walk with authority.

This mystery is about spiritual gifts: vision, prophecy, healing, discernment, and the ability to speak words that carry weight. In conjure, the Holy Spirit is what gives life to the work. A candle without Spirit is just wax and wick, but with Spirit it becomes a beacon. A prayer without Spirit is just words, but with Spirit it becomes command.

The Descent reminds us that Spirit does not stay distant; it comes down to fill jars of clay, everyday people, men and women, Black and white, enslaved and free. It is Spirit that empowers the powerless to stand. In Hoodoo tradition, this is the breath that wakes the bones, the shout that breaks chains, the fire that keeps away crossing and witchcraft meant to harm.

Keys for Prayer and Manifestation

For Spiritual Boldness: Pray for the courage to speak your truth, even if misunderstood.

For Divine Fire: Invite the Spirit to ignite your spiritual gifts and purpose.

For Protection of Energy: Remember that not everyone will recognize your anointing — guard your light.

For Higher Alignment: Use this mystery to rise above human opinion and move in the rhythm of Spirit.

Affirmations

I am filled with the Holy Spirit's fire and purpose.

I honor my divine experiences, even if others don't understand them.

The Spirit within me cannot be diminished by human opinion.

I operate in a wavelength of holiness that transcends misunderstanding.

The Assumption of Mary

(While Scripture does not narrate the Assumption directly, Catholic tradition and sacred art draw from passages like Revelation 12:1, Psalm 45:9 along with the Song of Songs and the typology of the Ark of the Covenant, to illuminate the mystery.)

Spiritual Meaning

The Assumption of Mary is a radiant proclamation of human potential. Just as Jesus ascended, Mary — fully human — was taken body and soul into heaven. This shows us that we do not need to be half divine in nature to rise into glory. What we need is the same "yes" Mary gave at the Annunciation — a life of openness to God, a steady walk in grace, and a heart aligned to divine will.

There is also a deeply intimate layer to this mystery: science affirms that mothers carry the DNA of their children within them. From this perspective, Mary carried within her the physical traces of Jesus for the rest of her life. Some may believe that it was this intimate bond — this indwelling presence of Christ — that drew her heavenward. And in a mystical sense, this applies to us too: when we "accept Jesus into our hearts", when we allow Christ's consciousness to live within us, we share in His destiny. We too can rise.

For Catholics, there is also a connection to the Eucharist. Receiving the Body of Christ — physically taking Him into ourselves — is seen as a foretaste of heaven, a pledge of our own resurrection. Even for those who experience Christ as already within them without the physical sacrament, the Assumption is a joyful promise: our humanity is not a limitation, but a vessel destined for divine union.

The Assumption is a victory after suffering — Mary's reward for a lifetime of faith, love, and steadfastness. It is a reminder that our story does not end in pain or loss, but in rising.

Hoodoo Insights

The Assumption reminds us that those who walk in goodness are not forgotten. Mary's body did not see decay because her life of grace, struggle, and devotion was honored and lifted up. In Hoodoo, this mystery connects deeply with the way we hold our ancestors: the ones who suffered, who lived through poverty, ridicule, and hardship, yet still carried themselves with quiet strength.

When you pray this decade, you can remember that our ancestors who lived well — even if the world never praised them — are seen, uplifted, and rewarded. Their goodness has not vanished into the dirt; it has risen and now watches over us from above.

The Assumption tells us that the dignity of a holy life does not go unnoticed. Just as Mary was carried into glory, so too are the spirits of our good ancestors raised up, their blessings continuing to flow to us.

When we live with love, when we strive for goodness, we are walking in their footsteps, and heaven itself takes note.

Each Hail Mary becomes a way of acknowledging that the ones who came before us are alive in Spirit, surrounding us, lifting us, cheering us on. It is a promise that hardship does not have the last word. Grace does. And in the end, like Mary, and like our ancestors who lived with quiet faith and courage, we too will be carried higher than the struggles of this world.

Keys for Prayer and Manifestation

For Spiritual Elevation: Call on Mary's example when you feel bound by earthly limitations.

For Union with the Divine: Pray to become more receptive to Christ's presence within you.

For Release and Rising: Let go of the weight of past wounds so your spirit can rise freely.

For Endurance: Trust that after trials, joy will come in full measure.

Affirmations

My humanity is a vessel for divine glory

I say "yes" to God's call and rise into higher states of being.

The presence of Christ within me draws me into union with God.

I am destined for light, joy, and eternal life.

The Coronation of Mary

And a great sign appeared in heaven: a woman clothed with the sun, with the moon under her feet, and on her head a crown of twelve stars." — **Revelation 12:1**

"You are the glory of Jerusalem, the joy of Israel; you are the fairest honor of our race." — **Judith 15:9**

Spiritual Meaning

The Coronation of Mary as Queen of Heaven is the divine seal on her life of "yes." She is crowned not only because she is the Mother of God but because she is the perfect disciple, the faithful servant who allowed her soul to be completely aligned with God's will. In her glorification, Mary becomes the Queen who reigns not by domination but by intercession, her authority flowing from love and her proximity to the King of Kings.

Her crown of twelve stars recalls the universality of her queenship—over all nations, all peoples, and every season of life. Mystically, these stars can be seen as the twelve signs of the zodiac, affirming that she moves through time and season with us, knowing every pattern and passage of the human journey. Her moon-cradled feet speak of mastery over emotions, illusions, and cycles that would otherwise control us. She is not only in heaven; she is sovereign over the very elements that shape our earthly lives.

Mary's coronation also offers a deeply personal message: she has gone before us to receive the crown of life promised to all who persevere in love and faith. She reigns not in isolation but as a model and companion, assuring us that in our own "yes" to God lies the path to glory. And as the New Eve, crowned and victorious, she crushes the serpent—showing that the temptations and lower impulses that once seduced humanity are no match for the woman fully united to God.

Hoodoo Insights

The Coronation of Mary as Queen of Heaven and Angels is a vision of what happens when grace, humility and perseverance are finally crowned. In Hoodoo, we understand crowns not only as symbols of authority but as signs that a life of endurance and dignity has been acknowledged by heaven and by the ancestors. Mary's coronation shows us that heaven raises up those the world has cast down. The same Spirit that lifted her up now works through the line of our ancestors. To walk with Mary crowned Queen is to walk knowing that we, too inherit crowns, crowns of spiritual victory, ancestral honor, and divine blessing.

Keys for Prayer and Manifestation

Crown Workings: Pray this mystery while holding or wearing a crown, headwrap, or headpiece anointed with blessing oil to magnetize honor, recognition, and divine favor.

Zodiac & Timing: Petition Mary during the sun's transit through your zodiac sign or during new/full moons in signs aligned to your intention (e.g., Leo for leadership, Pisces for spiritual vision).

Emotional Mastery: Use moon water, blessed under her image, to anoint your forehead and heart, asking her to bring emotional balance and sovereignty over reactive feelings.

Crushing the Serpent: Place your written temptations, anxieties, or recurring obstacles under a small statue or image of Mary with the serpent under her feet. Pray the Hail Holy Queen daily until you feel release.

Twelve-Star Petition: Write twelve intentions—one for each zodiac sign—on a paper star garland, hanging it in your prayer space to symbolize her blessing over every "season" of your life.

Affirmations

I reign with grace, crowned in divine favor.

Every season of my life is blessed and guided.

I master my emotions and walk in peace.

I am protected from temptation and strengthened in virtue.

My "yes" to God leads me to glory.

10

The Luminous Mysteries

The Luminous Mysteries—also called the Mysteries of Light—draw us into the public ministry of Jesus. They are the moments when His divinity shines forth openly, revealing His mission to the world. Instituted by Pope John Paul II in 2002, these mysteries invite us to contemplate Christ as the Light of the world, not hidden away in infancy or behind closed doors, but radiantly active among His people.

Where the Joyful Mysteries center on hidden beginnings and the Sorrowful Mysteries confront the cost of love, the Luminous Mysteries illuminate the active path of living out divine mission. They are filled with the brilliance of revelation—miracles, teachings, sacraments—moments when heaven's light bursts into the ordinary to make it extraordinary.

The addition of this set of mysteries, however, was not without discussion. Traditionally, the rosary's 150 Hail Marys were linked to the 150 Psalms, creating a prayer rhythm steeped in centuries of devotion. With the Luminous Mysteries added, that original symmetry is altered.

For this reason, some traditionalists do not pray them, holding to the original three sets of mysteries (Joyful, Sorrowful, and Glorious). Pope John Paul II himself introduced the Luminous Mysteries as optional, a gift to enrich prayer, not a replacement for the older structure.

In these mysteries, we witness the unveiling of the Kingdom of God. The waters of the Jordan open to reveal the Trinity. Water becomes wine at a wedding feast. The Good News is proclaimed with authority. The glory of the Transfiguration leaves the disciples awestruck and the Bread of Life is given as a pledge of eternal union.

The Luminous Mysteries remind us that the spiritual life is not only about beginnings or endings—it is about the living in-between. It is about how we embody divine light in our day-to-day lives, how we bring miracles into our relationships, and how we serve as vessels of truth and transformation.

In the sections that follow, we will walk through each Glorious Mystery with:

- The scriptural account of the event.
- Spiritual meanings and mystical layers.
- Keys for unlocking the power of each mystery in your life.
- Practical affirmations to carry the truth of each meditation into your daily walk.

The Baptism

"When Jesus was baptized, He went up immediately from the water, and behold, the heavens were opened to Him, and He saw the Spirit of God descending like a dove and coming to rest on Him; and behold, a voice from heaven said, 'This is my beloved Son, with whom I am well pleased.'" — **Matthew 3:16-17**

Spiritual Meaning

John the Baptist's entire mission was to prepare the way for Jesus. This mystery reminds us that before stepping fully into our divine calling, we too must prepare ourselves. Baptism—whether by water, prayer, or intentional spiritual cleansing—marks a crossing-over point. It is the washing away of what no longer serves and the readiness to receive more in our lives.

When Jesus came to the Jordan, it was not for repentance—He was sinless—but to model for us the posture of humility before the Father. As He rose from the waters, the heavens opened, the Spirit descended, and the Father's voice affirmed His identity. This shows us that when we step into our true purpose, we will receive unmistakable signs from God that we are exactly where we are meant to be.

This mystery also invites us to see preparation not as delay, but as sacred groundwork. The anointing, the signs, and the confirmations often come after we've taken the step of obedience. Like the Jordan River's flowing waters, the moment is alive, cleansing, and ready to carry you forward.

Hoodoo Insights

The Baptism of Jesus is more than a washing with water — it is an anointing, a claiming, and a revelation. In Hoodoo, we understand baptism not only as a church ritual but as a spiritual initiation. It marks the moment when the Spirit speaks, "This one is mine. This one carries my work."

In this mystery, when the heavens open and the Spirit descends, it reminds us of the ways our ancestors marked beginnings. They would bathe newborns in herbs, dress them with oils, and pray over them to set their lives on a good path. Baptism in this sense is both cleansing and sealing — cleansing away what clings, and sealing with blessing and purpose.

When you meditate on this mystery through the lens of Hoodoo, consider your own beginnings. What waters have you passed through? Who spoke your name into the world? Which ancestors prayed over you, even if silently, as you entered life's current?

This mystery also teaches that baptism is not about perfection, but about preparation. It doesn't mean your life will be without trials — even Jesus went straight from baptism into the wilderness. Instead, it is a reminder that when you are claimed by God, the ancestors, and Spirit, you do not walk alone. The heavens themselves take notice.

Keys for Prayer and Manifestation

Spiritual Cleansing: Before major life shifts, cleanse yourself spiritually—through baths, floor washes, or prayers—to make space for new blessings.

Ritual Anointing: Just as the Spirit descended on Jesus, use holy oil or blessed water to anoint your head and hands before prayer, symbolizing the sealing of your calling.

Affirm Your Readiness: Speak aloud your willingness to step into your divine purpose. Words are a powerful key in both hoodoo and mystical prayerwork.

Watch for Signs: Keep your eyes and spirit open for confirmations from God—through dreams, scripture, synchronicities, or encouragement from others—that you are on the right path.

Affirmations

> I am prepared for the blessings that are meant for me.
>
> I receive divine confirmation that I am exactly where I am meant to be.
>
> My spirit is cleansed and my heart is ready for my calling.
>
> God affirms me, the Spirit empowers me, and I walk forward with confidence.

The Wedding at Cana

"When the wine ran out, the mother of Jesus said to Him, 'They have no wine.' And Jesus said to her, 'Woman, what does this have to do with me? My hour has not yet come.' His mother said to the servants, 'Do whatever He tells you.' Jesus said to the servants, 'Fill the jars with water.' And they filled them up to the brim. When the master of the feast tasted the water now become wine... he said... 'You have kept the good wine until now.'" — **John 2:3-5, 7-10**

Spiritual Meaning

This mystery is a luminous jewel for understanding Mary's role as an intercessor. Here we see her perceive a need, bring it to Jesus, and arrange the circumstances for the miracle. She knew His purpose, His power, and His identity long before others fully realized it.

Even when Jesus said, "My hour has not yet come," Mary's confidence in Him never wavered. She moved in quiet authority, instructing the servants to obey Him—knowing that her request would be honored.

This moment reveals the intimate bond between Mother and Son, and how their united mission unfolds in real time.

Spiritually, this teaches us that Mary can intercede for us in the same way. She sees the lack, the needs, and the quiet desperation in our lives. She knows how to set the stage so that miracles can occur—turning water into wine, lack into abundance.

It is also a sign to those who question devotion to Mary: if you want to get close to Jesus, you can go through Mary. She is not a barrier; she is a bridge. This miracle is biblical proof that her role is not about taking glory from Christ but about pointing us toward Him and facilitating His work in our lives.

And for all of us, the alchemy of this mystery is a reminder that transformation is possible. What is common and ordinary in your life can be turned into something rare and exquisite. With divine grace, your "water" can become "wine."

Hoodoo Insights

The Wedding at Cana is the first miracle of Jesus, and it happens in a place of joy — a wedding feast, full of laughter, dancing, and community. This tells us something: miracles don't just happen in deserts and battlefields; they also happen at the table, in the kitchen, at a celebration among family and friends.

In Hoodoo, we know that spirit walks with us in every place, not just in the formal spaces of church. Ancestors bless our everyday gatherings — the meals, the dances, the laughter. Just as Mary interceded at Cana, so too do our ancestors and guides intercede for us in the unseen. They are working things out behind the veil, taking care of problems before we even realize they are problems.

The turning of water into wine also carries the lesson of transformation. Hoodoo is full of stories of transformation: bitter roots turned to medicine, plain coins turned to prosperity, tears turned to strength. Cana reminds us that Spirit has the power to elevate what is common into what is blessed.

And there's a deeper comfort here: when we are in good spirits, when we are living with joy and openness, heaven and the ancestors look out for us. We don't need to carry every worry on our own. Just as the wedding guests had no idea how close they were to running out of wine — yet Mary and Jesus ensured they lacked nothing — so too are we shielded and supplied by those who walk with us in spirit.

To pray this mystery with Hoodoo eyes is to say: "I can rest, I can rejoice, I can dance. My ancestors see me. My guides prepare the way. What I lack is being filled even before I notice the cup is empty."

Keys for Prayer and Manifestation

Intercessory Petitioning: Pray to Mary for specific needs, trusting that she can present them to Jesus in the way that opens the door for divine action.

Obedience as a Catalyst: Like the servants who obeyed, follow the divine instructions you are given—miracles often happen through simple obedience.

Symbolic Water-to-Wine Workings: In hoodoo and folk magic, you can transform an item (like plain water) into something sweet or fragrant while praying this mystery, symbolizing the shift from lack to abundance.

Confidence in Timing: Even if it "is not yet your hour," trust that the request you've placed before heaven is being arranged for perfect timing.

Affirmations

I trust Mary to intercede for me and bring my needs to Jesus.

I am open to divine transformation in my life.

Lack in my life is being turned into abundance.

I follow divine instructions and witness miracles unfold.

The Proclamation of the Kingdom

"The time is fulfilled, and the kingdom of God is at hand; repent and believe in the gospel." — **Mark 1:15**

"Jesus went throughout all the cities and villages, teaching in their synagogues and proclaiming the gospel of the kingdom and healing every disease and every affliction." — **Matthew 9:35**

Spiritual Meaning

When Jesus proclaimed the Kingdom, He was not just making a bold statement about who He was—He was proving it. His ministry was not empty words; it was lived truth, embodied in miracles and physical manifestations that directly transformed people's daily lives. This was no longer just about turning water into wine for a single event; this was about radically changing the trajectory of someone's entire life.

And that made Him dangerous to the powers that be. His healings, His deliverances, and His truth-telling did not just inspire faith—they threatened the existing religious hierarchy. When Christ is truly active in a life, there will be a change. Addictions break. Chains fall off. Long-standing ailments or oppressive situations lift. While not every sickness disappears and not every struggle vanishes overnight, the hold of those burdens is broken. The Kingdom isn't simply about a future Heaven—it is a transformation that begins now, in tangible, undeniable ways.

To proclaim the Kingdom, then, is to stand in that same authority and to bring God's reality into the present moment—not just in words, but in ways that make people say, "My life will never be the same."

Hoodoo Insights

When Jesus proclaims the Kingdom, He is declaring that divine order and divine justice are already breaking into the world. In Hoodoo, we know that this kind of proclamation isn't just words—it's power. It's a spoken decree that changes the air, shifts the atmosphere, and opens the way for Spirit to move.

Our elders knew the power of a word spoken with authority. A prayer, a psalm, a spell—these were proclamations of a kingdom that the world didn't want to recognize but could not deny. When enslaved ancestors prayed in the hush arbors, they were proclaiming the Kingdom. When mothers prayed the Psalms over their children at night, they were proclaiming the Kingdom. Each declaration was a way of saying: Spirit rules here, not bondage. God rules here, not oppression. Justice rules here, not cruelty.

In Hoodoo, to proclaim is to align your tongue with heaven. The Kingdom is present when you declare over your life that you are free, that your family is covered, that your work is blessed. The Proclamation reminds us that the Kingdom is not somewhere far away—it is right here, wherever we stand and call down Spirit with faith, respect, and power.

Keys for Prayer and Manifestation

Proof in the Action: Pair spoken prayer with a tangible act—give, heal, clean, or bless as a physical sign of the Kingdom manifesting.

Breaking Chains Work: Use Psalm 107 in your prayer while anointing yourself or a symbol of the burden you wish to break, declaring freedom.

Atmosphere of Change: Light incense or diffuse oils associated with joy and renewal while proclaiming "The Kingdom is here."

Prophetic Gesture: Stand at your doorway and speak blessings over your home and neighborhood, marking your territory as Kingdom ground.

Affirmations

The Kingdom of God is active in my life right now.

I live in the proof, not just the proclamation.

What once held me no longer has power over me.

My presence brings the atmosphere of Heaven wherever I go.

The Transfiguration

"And He was transfigured before them, and His face shone like the sun, and His clothes became white as light." — **Matthew 17:2**

Spiritual Meaning

The Transfiguration shows us what happens when you are living fully in your purpose, in the presence of trusted companions, and in an elevated state—whether that's a literal mountain or a higher consciousness. Jesus brings Peter, James, and John to this high place, and in their company, He radiates His divine light. His guides—Moses and Elijah—appear, showing that when you are aligned, your ancestors, spiritual allies, and higher beings will meet you halfway.

This was not a public display for the masses, though He could have chosen that. Instead, it was an intimate revelation among those who could receive it. That reminds us in mystical practice that divine encounters and the most profound spiritual manifestations are often reserved for those moments when we are in the right place, at the right vibration, with the right people.

Hoodoo Insights

In Hoodoo and mystical work, you don't expect the heavens to open if you aren't willing to climb your own mountain—physically, mentally, or spiritually. To glow with your highest brilliance, you must prepare yourself, raise your energy, and meet the Divine halfway. This mystery is an invitation: if you want your light to shine and your guides to show up, get yourself to that high place where they can meet you.

Keys for Prayer and Manifestation

Light Workings: Pray Psalm 27 ("The Lord is my light and my salvation") over a white candle to amplify inner radiance.

Mountain Magic: Take your prayers to a literal high place, or use meditation to ascend to a higher consciousness.

Trusted Circle: Create spiritual gatherings only with those who uplift and understand you—your own "Peter, James, and John."

Ancestral Access: Before ritual, call on ancestors or guides you trust, inviting them to appear in your sacred space.

Affirmations

> I shine brightest when I am in my purpose and with my trusted circle.
>
> My guides and ancestors meet me at my highest vibration.
>
> I am worthy of private, sacred revelations from the Divine.

I climb my mountain and meet Heaven halfway.

The Eucharist

And He took bread, gave thanks and broke it, and gave it to them, saying, "This is my body given for you; do this in remembrance of me." In the same way, after the supper he took the cup, saying, "This cup is the new covenant in my blood, which is poured out for you." — **Luke 22:19-20**

Spiritual Meaning

In this mystery, Jesus gives us the greatest gift of His earthly ministry — Himself — under the humble appearance of bread and wine. This is not just a symbolic gesture; it is a covenant act, a divine exchange. By commanding His disciples to "do this in remembrance of me," He is not simply asking for memorial; He is inviting us to continually unite ourselves to Him through this sacred act until His work is complete.

Hoodoo Insights

When Jesus gives His Body and Blood to the disciples, He is not only feeding them—He is binding them into covenant. In Hoodoo, meals are never just meals; food is a way of transferring spirit, love, and blessing. Our ancestors knew that to sit at the table was to share more than bread—it was to share life itself.

The Eucharist reminds us that God can hide divine power in the simplest things—bread, wine, a table. Hoodoo recognizes this too: a glass of water on the altar, a bit of bread broken in prayer, wine poured as an offering—these carry Spirit. When we eat and drink with intention, we are joining into a mystery much bigger than us.

The Hoodoo way of seeing the Eucharist is that it binds us not just to Christ, but to each other, and to all our ancestors who fed us with their labor, their prayers, their endurance. Every time we partake, we join in a river of strength that flows through them to us.

Keys for Prayer and Manifestation

Feed the Work: Just as bread and wine nourish the body, continually nourish your prayers and workings until completion.

Sacred Remembrance: Return to your altar, your prayers, and your commitments consistently; absence weakens the current.

Embodiment: The Eucharist is not just something you take; it is something you become. Carry that divine presence into your daily life.

Unbroken Energy: Maintain the vibration until the "coming" of the promise, whether that is spiritual fulfillment or a specific life manifestation.

Affirmations

I keep my faith and energy steady until the work is complete.

I am nourished by the divine, and I embody its presence in all I do.

I feed my prayers and workings with love, focus, and unwavering belief.

My manifestations are sustained until they come to full fruition.

11

Praying the Rosary with Intention

In Hoodoo tradition, we often align our prayers with a purpose — a work. The mysteries themselves are already rich in symbolism, and each can be paired with a particular area of life where you may need blessing, movement, or change.

This is not about replacing the original meaning of the mysteries, but about layering your intentions into them — the same way we might dress a candle or write a petition. By meditating on the events of Jesus' and Mary's lives with a specific Hoodoo aim in mind, you are weaving your need into the fabric of your prayer.

Matching Mysteries to Your Petition

Below is a guide to pairing some traditional mysteries with common Hoodoo goals:

For Friendship, Favor, and Connection

The Visitation (Joyful Mysteries) — Mary's visit to Elizabeth is a lesson in mutual upliftment and divine connection. Pray this decade when you seek to make new friends, be welcomed into a new community, or strengthen bonds.

For Prophetic Dreams and Spirit Guidance

The Flight into Egypt (Joyful Mysteries) — Joseph's dream warned him to protect his family. Pray this when you desire clear spiritual messages, dreams, or visions that lead you to safety, opportunity, or purpose.

For Success in a New Venture

The Presentation in the Temple (Joyful Mysteries) — Jesus is publicly acknowledged in his purpose. Use this when launching a new project, ministry, or business to receive blessing and recognition.

For Courage to Face Challenges

The Agony in the Garden (Sorrowful Mysteries) — Jesus models how to surrender to divine will while facing hardship. Pray this when you need strength to endure and the courage to follow through.

For Financial Breakthroughs

The Wedding at Cana (Luminous Mysteries) — Mary's intercession turns lack into abundance. Pray this for provision, resources, and to see impossible situations change in your favor.

For Justice and Vindication

The Carrying of the Cross (Sorrowful Mysteries) — Christ's endurance through public humiliation is powerful for those facing injustice, slander, or legal trouble.

For Spiritual Elevation

The Transfiguration (Luminous Mysteries) — A vision of divine glory shared with trusted witnesses. Pray this when you seek to ascend spiritually, strengthen your gifts, or step fully into your higher calling.

For Healing

The Proclamation of the Kingdom of God (Luminous Mysteries) — Jesus changes lives with word and deed. Pray this for inner and outer healing, release from harmful patterns, and life transformation.

Why This Works

Each mystery holds layers of meaning that can be tuned toward your intention. The Bible stories themselves contain archetypal energies — journeys, miracles, trials, victories — that resonate with specific outcomes in your life. If you meditate upon them and feel it happening during your contemplation of them you are magically calling this energy into your life. When you see and feel Mary's joy upon seeing Elizabeth you are inviting joy and sisterhood into your own life. In addition, when you prayerfully contemplate on applicable mysteries, the answers and next steps will be revealed to you during your prayers. The mysteries begin to communicate with you.

What Comes Next

In the next chapter, we will explore how to combine these intentional meditations with ritual work. This includes choosing a rosary, preparing it for spiritual use, and integrating traditional Hoodoo methods such as cleansing, dressing, and petitioning — all while keeping the heart of the rosary intact as a sacred conversation with Mary, the saints, and God.

12

The Rosary as a Magical Tool

Now that you know what the prayers are, you've explored the mysteries, and you've likely prayed the rosary a few times, you can begin using the rosary as a working tool within hoodoo. This isn't about abandoning its devotional power — in fact, devotion is the foundation. But you can also use the rosary for petition work: asking Mary, the angels, and the saints for specific help.

A rosary in this context becomes both an offering and a conduit. It's not only a chain of beads for meditating on sacred mysteries — it's a tangible instrument for directing your intentions, building spiritual relationships, and pulling down blessings into the physical world.

Grace Through Devotion Alone

Before I began actively vocalizing my petitions, I went through a season where I prayed the rosary every single day for weeks — purely out of love and devotion to Mary. I wasn't asking for anything specific. I wasn't even thinking about magic or manifestation.

And yet, without me ever putting my requests into words, I began to see shifts. Opportunities opened up. Obstacles softened. Blessings flowed into my life in ways I hadn't anticipated.

That's the nature of grace: when you consistently pray the rosary from the heart, you are building a living relationship with Mary and the holy energies she is connected to. This relationship alone can begin to realign your life. In some cases, you may find that simply keeping this devotional practice brings about the changes you thought you'd need to formally petition for.

It Doesn't Have to Be Ritual-Heavy

It's not necessary to go through elaborate rituals in order to work with the rosary. Of course, you can ritualize everything — bring out the candles, the herbs, the oils, set prayers, and intentional work — but hoodoo has always been about using what you have.

If you only have a few quiet moments, a simple rosary in your hands, and your voice, that is enough. If you have time and materials to add layers of ritual, you can. But do not think that a lack of props nor a perfectly staged altar will prevent you from working with these energies. Spirit meets you where you are.

A Universal Practice

Prayer beads are not exclusive to Catholicism. They appear in spiritual traditions across the world:

African Diasporic Traditions – Cowrie shells, seeds, and beads strung for divination, ancestor veneration, and protective charms.

Islamic Tasbih – 99 or 33 beads used to recite the names of Allah and devotional phrases.

Buddhist & Hindu Mala – 108 beads (plus a guru bead) for repeating mantras during meditation.

Eastern Orthodox Prayer Rope (Chotki or Komboskini) – Knotted cord, often with 33, 50, or 100 knots, used to repeat the Jesus Prayer.

Anglican Rosary – A modern adaptation of the Catholic rosary, with 33 beads symbolizing the years of Christ's life.

Pagan Prayer Beads – Beads aligned with lunar phases, seasonal festivals, or deities, used in spellwork and meditation.

Historically, lay Christians used beads to connect spiritually with monks and friars who prayed the 150 Psalms — the rosary being a devotional echo of those prayers. You can keep to that lineage or deviate entirely, letting your beads serve your personal, spiritual, and magical practice.

Choosing the Right Rosary for Your Work

Your choice of rosary can align with the intention of your petition:

By Color:

- White or blue: Marian devotion, peace, healing, purity

- Green: Prosperity, growth, and steady success

- Red: Passion, protection, justice

- Black: Banishing, ancestral work, protection from harm

By Material:

- Wood: Earthy grounding, ancestral connection

- Glass or crystal beads: Amplification of intention, clarity

- Precious stones: Bring in the stone's metaphysical properties (e.g., rose quartz for love)

The material and color of your rosary help to "tune" it toward your goal.

Preparing Your Rosary for Petition Work

Just like any working tool in hoodoo, the rosary can be cleansed, charged, and dressed for specific workings:

1. Cleanse — Pass your rosary through incense or sprinkle it lightly with blessed water.

2. Charge — Hold it while visualizing your intention, allowing your energy and focus to soak into the beads.

3. Dress — Lightly anoint with appropriate oil (e.g., frankincense for prayer, rose for love, protection oil for defense).

Important Notes Before Petitioning

Some of the spirits we call on — Mary, angels, saints — cannot be bribed. They do not require offerings to help you, but relationship matters.

From my own practice, I've found that you will receive faster, more profound results — often beyond your wildest expectations — if you show you are genuinely here to build a relationship. That means speaking to them daily, offering thanks before you see results. and being open to their timing and the bigger plan.

Petitioning without relationship can feel transactional — and while your request may still be heard, it will lack the depth and mutual trust that unlocks miraculous results.

13

Working the Rosary

Before we get into the steps, I want to speak from my heart about something important: your confidence and comfort with your rosary matter more than following anyone else's "rules."

I've heard people say you should never use a rosary if you don't know where it came from, or that you should only work with brand-new beads. I don't agree. If a rosary calls out to you—whether it's brand new in a shop, found in a thrift store, or passed down from a family member—trust that connection. In fact, if you have an heirloom rosary that belonged to a powerful praying grandmother or another ancestor, that's not something to fear; that's a blessing. Those beads have been bathed in prayer.

Do I personally have certain rosaries dedicated to specific devotions? Yes. I have one for Our Lady Untier of Knots that I go to when I need to break through obstacles, and others that I keep purely for devotional work. But if you don't have the means, space, or desire to collect multiple rosaries, that's okay. You can pray and petition powerfully with the one you have.

While cleansing, charging, or dressing your rosary can be a beautiful way to prepare for ritual, don't feel bound by formality. If your only option in the moment is to take the beads you already have on hand and start praying—do it. The rosary itself, prayed with sincerity, can move mountains.

Quick Guide to a Rosary Petition Ritual

1. Set Your Petition

Write down your request in 1–2 clear sentences.

- Example: "I ask Our Lady to open the way for peace in my home."

2. Choose the Rosary

Select a color and material matching your intention.

- Green = prosperity, Blue = peace, Black = protection.

3. Prepare the Space

Clean, quiet area.

- Optional: candle, water, incense, oil.

4. Cleanse the Rosary (optional)

Pass through incense, sprinkle with blessed water, or pray over the beads.

5. Charge the Rosary

Hold it, visualize your petition as already granted.

6. (Optional) Dress the Rosary

Anoint the crucifix or center medal with appropriate oil.

7. Pray the Rosary

Pray as normal, pausing between decades to repeat your petition.

8. Give Thanks

End with a prayer of gratitude as if your petition is fulfilled.

9. Seal the Work

Let candles burn out safely, make the sign of the cross, store the rosary respectfully.

10. Act in the Physical

Take real-world steps to support your request.

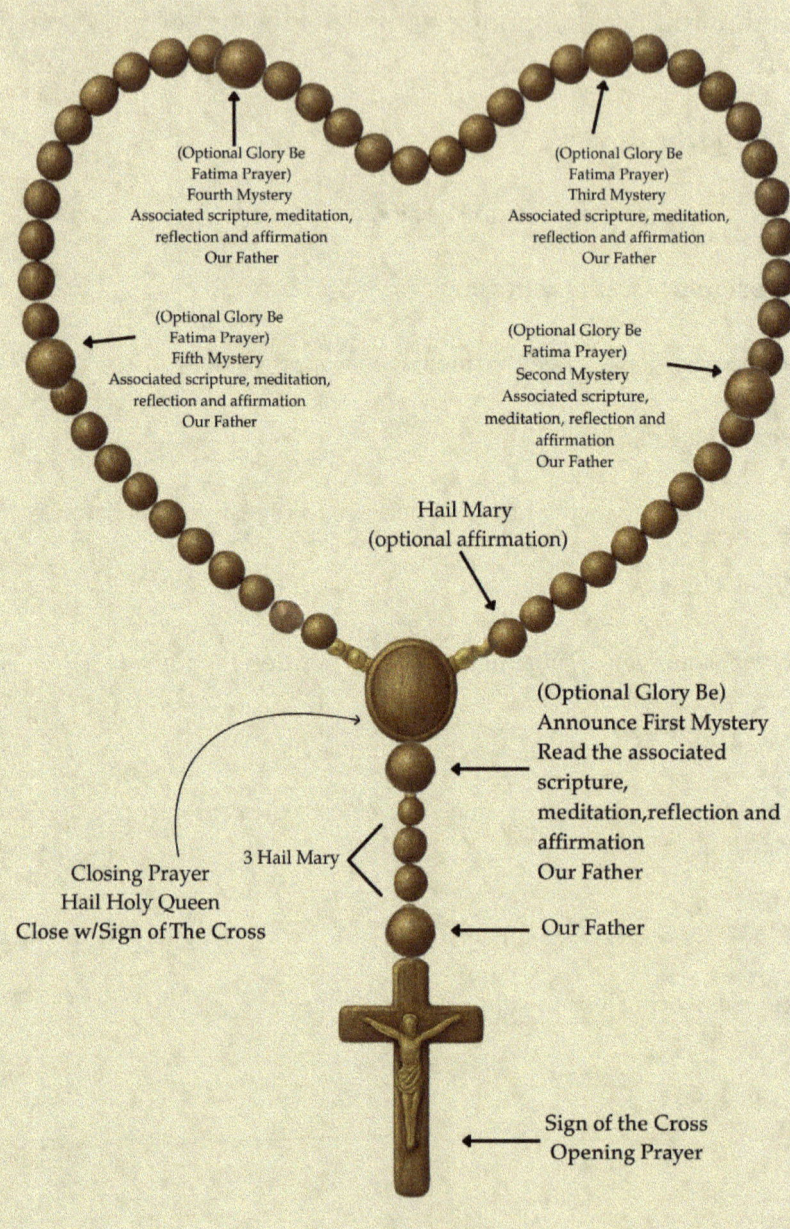

14

Praying the Rosary for Specific Needs

After you've learned the prayers, meditated on the mysteries, and explored ritualizing your rosary work, you can begin to shape the rosary toward specific areas of your life. You may choose to stick with the traditional mysteries exactly as they are — and this alone will bless many areas of your life. But you also have the freedom to adapt the structure to focus on a single intention or life challenge.

In my own practice, I have found that the rosary is not locked to only one set of meditations. I've prayed it using different Bible verses, stories, and characters as the core of each decade. Sometimes, a mystery from the life of a prophet, a psalm, or even a parable will speak directly to what I'm facing. Those become my meditations, and the rosary becomes my way of weaving those lessons into my spirit. That for me is the Hoodoo Rosary.

Keeping the Structure, Adjusting the Focus

The power of the rosary is in its rhythm — the beads, the prayers, and the repetition that builds spiritual energy. You can keep that structure while adjusting what you say and meditate on:

Using the Traditional Hail Mary

The Hail Mary is the heart of the rosary and will always connect you to Mary's intercession. Many days, I stick to the Hail Mary on every bead while focusing my mind on my chosen intention.

Swapping the Hail Mary for Affirmations

Once you've built a relationship with Mary, she takes no offense to you praying affirmations instead of the Hail Mary on certain occasions. I have done this myself — each bead becomes an affirmation in line with my goal, such as:

"I am walking in divine favor."

"My path is clear and blessed."

"I am surrounded by protection and grace."

Blending the Two

You can alternate — praying a Hail Mary on one bead, then an affirmation on the next, or even recite the two one after the other on each individual bead.

Bible Verses as Decade Meditations

Another way to personalize your rosary for specific work is to choose a Bible verse for each decade that supports your intention. For example:

- Praying for guidance? Meditate on Proverbs 3:5–6.
- Seeking healing? Meditate on Isaiah 53:5.
- Asking for courage? Meditate on Joshua 1:9.

The beads hold your focus, while the verse shapes your mind and energy toward the desired outcome.

Freedom Within Tradition

The rosary has been prayed in many ways by many people across time. In Hoodoo, we honor what works — what is effective and moves results. You can be deeply traditional or beautifully adaptive. What matters most is your sincerity, your relationship with Mary and the divine, and your consistency in prayer.

Money Drawing & Abundance Rosary

Over time, I've learned something important in my relationship with Mary: I don't really go to her for quick-cash workings. Not because she can't bring them — she absolutely can — but because I've found that the way she moves in my life with money is different from that. She works in a way that already knows what I need before I even speak it. She sends it through unexpected channels, through other people, and in ways that don't require me to grind myself down or make sacrifices that drain me.

In my experience, Mary's money blessings are long-term and foundational. They're about true abundance, about creating good financial standing and stability that lasts — the kind that can ripple out to your children and grandchildren. She will align the right opportunities, put the right people in your path, and ensure your table is never empty.

If you're seeking generational wealth, steady income, and the fullness of an abundant life, I cannot recommend working with her enough. But if you're in urgent need of immediate cash — rent due tomorrow, a bill collector calling — you may find a better fit in working with a different energy alongside your prayers, such as Saint Expedite, who is well known for swiftness in financial miracles.

Of course, there are Marian titles that lean toward the more urgent side of help — Our Lady of Perpetual Help, Our Lady of Prompt Succor

— and you can absolutely call on them for faster results. Still, in my own relationship with Mary, the abundance she brings has always been purposeful, often arriving in ways I didn't think to ask for, and never just "to prove" she can bring me money. Her wealth is the wealth of a mother who ensures her children will be cared for, clothed, fed, and set on firm ground.

This rosary is for inviting in that kind of abundance — the abundance that sustains, grows roots, and expands beyond you.

Opening Prayer

Blessed Mother Mary, Queen of Heaven and Earth, I come before you with a humble heart, seeking the blessings of divine provision. Intercede for me before your Son, that my work may prosper, my hands be blessed, and my table overflow with good things. May every dollar I touch be clean, righteous, and multiplied for the good of my life and the lives I bless. Holy Spirit, guide my thoughts toward wisdom, my actions toward increase, and my heart toward gratitude. Amen.

First Decade – God as the Source of All Provision

"The LORD will open for you the heavens, the storehouse of His bounty, to send rain on your land in season and to bless all the work of your hands." – **Deuteronomy 28:12**

Meditation: See the storehouse of heaven opening above you, pouring out blessings in perfect timing.

Reflection: What does it feel like to truly trust that my provision comes from God?

Affirmation: "I am connected to the Source of all abundance. My work is blessed, and increase comes to me now."

Hoodoo Correspondence: Psalm: 65 (for drawing blessings and favor) Candle Color: Green Oil: Money Drawing or Prosperity Oil Herb: Cinnamon (quick increase) Working Idea: Light a green candle dressed with oil and cinnamon before praying.

Second Decade – Overflowing Cup

"My cup overflows. Surely goodness and mercy shall follow me all the days of my life." – **Psalm 23:5-6**

Meditation: Imagine your cup being filled until it overflows — not with just enough, but with more than enough to share.

Reflection: Where can I open my heart to overflow, instead of living from fear or lack?

Affirmation: "I am blessed to be a blessing. My overflow blesses me and those I love."

Hoodoo Correspondence: Psalm: 23 (for abundance and blessings) Candle Color: Gold Oil: Crown of Success Oil Herb: Chamomile (draws money and luck) Working Idea: Brew chamomile tea and wash your hands in it before handling money.

Third Decade – The Work of Your Hands

"May the favor of the Lord our God rest on us; establish the work of our hands for us—yes, establish the work of our hands." – **Psalm 90:17**

Meditation: See your hands glowing with divine light as you work. Every task you do draws in wealth, respect, and opportunity.

Reflection: How can I approach my work with gratitude and sacred intention, even in small tasks?

Affirmation: "The work of my hands is holy. It draws prosperity to me with ease."

Hoodoo Correspondence: Psalm: 90 (for blessing work and labor) Candle Color: Yellow Oil: Fast Luck Oil Herb: Alfalfa (keeps money in the home) Working Idea: Place alfalfa in your wallet or cash drawer while praying this decade.

Fourth Decade – Pressed Down, Shaken Together

"Give, and it will be given to you. A good measure, pressed down, shaken together, and running over, will be poured into your lap." – **Luke 6:38**

Meditation: Feel yourself receiving a generous, overflowing measure — abundance beyond your expectations.

Reflection: How does generosity open the doors for my own blessings?

Affirmation: "As I give freely, so I receive freely. My abundance runs over."

Hoodoo Correspondence: Psalm: 112 (prosperity and generosity) Candle Color: White or Gold Oil: Blessing Oil Herb: Basil (prosperity and protection) Working Idea: Sprinkle basil water around your home to draw blessings.

Fifth Decade – The God Who Provides

"And my God will meet all your needs according to the riches of his glory in Christ Jesus." – **Philippians 4:19**

Meditation: Picture your needs met with divine elegance and perfect timing, without strain or struggle.

Reflection: Am I ready to believe my needs are already met?

Affirmation: "I live in divine supply. All my needs are met now and always."

Hoodoo Correspondence: Psalm: 34 (help in need, attracting good things) Candle Color: Green and Gold (double action) Oil: Attraction Oil Herb: Bay Leaf (write your petition and place under candle) Working Idea: Burn a green-and-gold candle over a petition on a bay leaf while praying.

Closing Prayer

Mother Mary, intercede for me that I may always walk in abundance without pride, in prosperity without greed, and in blessing without fear. May I use my wealth for good, to honor God and uplift others. I thank you now for the miracles of provision already on their way. Amen.

Power and Command Rosary

There's a misconception about Christianity — especially Catholicism — that it's about being meek, submissive, and powerless. I believe this comes from the way many people have only witnessed faith through certain clergy, priests, or nuns who have adopted an "I am weak, I am nothing, I am a sinner" posture. But when you actually open the Bible — truly read it — the message is not one of weakness. It's one of empowerment.

Scripture tells us we are made in the image of God. Jesus Himself said that the works He did, we would do also — and greater. That power is not reserved for the saints in stained glass; it's in you. If it feels dormant, you can ask the Holy Spirit to awaken it.

When we come to Mary in devotion, yes, we're asking for intercession — but that's not because we are groveling in unworthiness. It's like going to an elder in Hoodoo: we show respect, not because we think we don't belong in the same room, but because we honor the wisdom and connection they carry.

Hoodoo has always been about power — the God-given, inborn authority to change our lives and our circumstances. Our African-American ancestors practiced it in the face of oppression, hardship, and every system designed to strip them of power, yet they remained spiritually unbreakable.

The Power & Command Rosary is about remembering who you are, reclaiming your voice, and standing in the authority God has placed in you. True Christianity and true Hoodoo both call you to be unafraid of your gifts, unafraid of your brilliance, and unafraid to take your rightful place in the world.

Opening Prayer

Mother Mary, who crushes the serpent's head, intercessor and warrior of the faithful, I come to this rosary seeking holy authority — the authority to stand in my purpose, to command my craft, to move in the will of God without hesitation. With the strength of Christ and the wisdom of the Spirit, may my words carry weight, my prayers be heard, and my steps be steady in every battle. Amen.

First Decade – Speaking with Authority

"For the Spirit God gave us does not make us timid, but gives us power, love, and self-discipline." – **2 Timothy 1:7**

Meditation: When you speak, speak as one who carries Heaven's endorsement. Your voice is a tool of creation, blessing, and decree.

Reflection: Where in your life have you been silent when you should have spoken? Where have you let others speak over you instead of declaring your own vision?

Affirmation: I speak with the voice of truth. My words carry power and shift the atmosphere.

Hoodoo Correspondences: Psalm 29 (The voice of the Lord is powerful) Candle Color: Red or purple Herb: Calamus root (for commanding speech), licorice root (for influence) Working Idea: Pray this decade while holding your rosary over a glass of water, then drink the water to "take in" the command you've just spoken.

Second Decade – Authority Over Your Path

"I will give you every place where you set your foot, as I promised Moses." – **Joshua 1:3**

Meditation: Step into spaces knowing they belong to you by divine appointment. Your presence is not by accident — it is anointed.

Reflection: Are there places you've been afraid to go, rooms you've been afraid to enter? Why?

Affirmation: Every space I step into is claimed for my purpose.

Hoodoo Correspondences: Psalm 37:23–24 (The steps of a good man are ordered by the Lord) Candle Color: Brown or gold Herb: Gravel root (to remove obstacles from your path) Working Idea: Pray while walking your property or neighborhood, claiming each step.

Third Decade – Command in the Spiritual Realm

"See, I have given you authority to tread on snakes and scorpions and over all the power of the enemy; nothing will harm you." – **Luke 10:19**

Meditation: You have power over spiritual attacks. Stand firm knowing you are equipped for every battle.

Reflection: Do you hesitate to pray boldly against what comes against you?

Affirmation: I move in divine authority. No weapon formed against me prospers.

Hoodoo Correspondences: Psalm 91 (Protection and authority) Candle Color: Black (for banishing) with a white candle for divine authority Herb: Angelica root (holy protection and command) Working Idea: Dress your rosary with protective oil before praying this decade.

Fourth Decade – Command Over Your Craft

"Do you see someone skilled in their work? They will serve before kings." – **Proverbs 22:29**

Meditation: Your craft — whether spiritual work, art, or business — is a gift from God. Move in confidence and refine your skill until your work speaks for you.

Reflection: Have you been holding back your skill or power for fear of being "too much"?

Affirmation: I am skilled, confident, and my work opens doors before me.

Hoodoo Correspondences: Psalm 90:17 (May the favor of the Lord establish the work of our hands) Candle Color: Yellow (for mastery) or orange (for attraction) Herb: Master root (for mastery in craft) Working Idea: Keep your rosary near your tools of craft while praying this decade.

Fifth Decade – Standing as a Leader

"The Lord will make you the head, not the tail." – **Deuteronomy 28:13**

Meditation: Leadership is not domination — it is responsibility, vision, and service guided by divine wisdom.

Reflection: Where in your life is God calling you to lead, but you've been reluctant to step forward?

Affirmation: I am the head and not the tail. I lead with power, wisdom, and grace.

Hoodoo Correspondences: Psalm 20 (Victory and success for leaders) Candle Color: Purple (for leadership and dignity) Herb: High John the Conqueror root (for victory and commanding respect) Working Idea: Pray over a High John root while doing this decade, then carry it with you as a pocket charm.

Closing Prayer

Mary, Queen of Heaven, and all the saints and angels who walk in authority, help me to step fully into my purpose, to speak with confidence, to act with wisdom, and to command my craft with integrity. May every gift I've been given be used to glorify God and to lift others into their own divine authority. Amen.

Protection Rosary

From my own practice, I've found that praying the rosary — especially with protection in mind — has deepened my connection to both Saint Michael and the Virgin Mary. With that connection comes an undeniable sense of their presence, their guardianship, and the comfort of always seeing signs that they are with me.

Through the rosary, I've developed sharper spiritual discernment. I avoid risky situations almost instinctively now, as if guided away before I even step into them. It feels as though there's an aura around me — a constant, invisible shield — born of consecrating myself to the angels and to Mary.

In this way, I've become what I call a living prayer. I am always protected.

Before I began consistently praying the rosary, I would often feel the need to "refresh" my wards or repeat protection spells. Now, the very act of praying the rosary — meditating on these psalms, invoking the mysteries, and calling on the intercession of the Holy Ones — is itself a continual reinforcement of my spiritual shield. Each prayer is a fresh cloak of protection, each decade a renewed covering beneath Mary's mantle, each word a strengthening of the fiery wall that Saint Michael guards.

With that in mind, the Protection Rosary you are about to pray is more than just a set of beads and words — it is an active spiritual armor. As you work through each decade, you are layering that shield, brick by brick, flame by flame, until you are standing firmly within the fiery wall of protection and the blessed mantle of Our Lady.

Opening Prayer

Blessed Mother Mary, wrap me in your mantle of protection.

Saint Michael the Archangel, defend me in battle; be my safeguard against the wickedness and snares of the enemy.

Lord God, set Your fiery wall around me, my home, my loved ones, and all that You have entrusted to me.

Let no harm come near, let no curse take root, and let no evil cross my threshold.

Amen.

First Decade — Psalm 91:1-2

"He who dwells in the shelter of the Most High will rest in the shadow of the Almighty. I will say of the Lord, 'He is my refuge and my fortress, my God, in whom I trust.'"

Meditation: God's presence is a fortress. Mary is the sheltering mantle. Saint Michael is the sword at the door. You are safe.

Reflection: Where in your life do you need to truly rest in God's shadow?

Affirmation: I dwell in divine shelter and no harm can find me.

Hoodoo Correspondences: Psalm: 91 Candle Color: White (purity, light) Herbs: Angelica root, Rue Working Idea: Light a white candle dressed with Van Van oil while praying this decade for clearing away spiritual debris.

Second Decade — Isaiah 54:17

"No weapon that is formed against you shall prosper, and every tongue that shall rise against you in judgment you shall condemn."

Meditation: The fiery wall is up — no weapon can cross it, no lie can stick.

Reflection: Whose words or actions have you allowed to pierce your spirit?

Affirmation: No weapon against me will prosper — I am shielded by God's fire.

Hoodoo Correspondences: Psalm: 35 Candle Color: Red (fiery wall) Herbs: Cinnamon, Dragon's Blood Working Idea: Dress a red candle with Fiery Wall of Protection oil and pray this decade while visualizing fire surrounding your home.

Third Decade — Luke 10:19

"Behold, I have given you authority to tread on serpents and scorpions, and over all the power of the enemy; and nothing shall hurt you."

Meditation: You have spiritual authority — nothing has permission to harm you.

Reflection: What harmful patterns or attacks have you allowed authority over you?

Affirmation: I walk in authority and nothing can harm me.

Hoodoo Correspondences: Psalm: 140 Candle Color: Blue (peace, divine authority) Herbs: Bay leaf, Basil Working Idea: Place bay leaves in the four corners of your home while praying this decade to mark your territory as untouchable.

Fourth Decade — Ephesians 6:11

"Put on the whole armor of God, so that you may be able to stand against the schemes of the devil."

Meditation: The armor of God is your constant clothing; you are never unprotected.

Reflection: Where do you still feel spiritually vulnerable?

Affirmation: I am clothed in God's armor — nothing can break through.

Hoodoo Correspondences: Psalm: 121 Candle Color: Gold (divine light) Herbs: Hyssop, Frankincense Working Idea: Wash your doorway with hyssop tea while praying this decade to cleanse and protect all who enter.

Fifth Decade — Revelation 12:7-8

"Now war arose in heaven, Michael and his angels fighting against the dragon. And the dragon and his angels fought back, but they were defeated."

Meditation: The battle is already won; Saint Michael fights for you now.

Reflection: What "dragons" in your life need to be cast down?

Affirmation: Saint Michael defends me and victory is already mine.

Hoodoo Correspondences: Psalm: 34 Candle Color: Purple (authority, power) Herbs: Black Cohosh, Clove Working Idea: Carry a pinch of clove in a mojo bag for ongoing protection while praying this decade.

Closing Prayer

Blessed Mother, Queen of Heaven, shield me beneath your mantle.

Saint Michael, defend me day and night.

God Almighty, keep the fiery wall blazing around me.

May every path I walk be clear, Every gate be guarded, And every shadow turned into light.

Amen.

Road-Opener Rosary

This is one of my favorite rosaries to pray outdoors, especially while walking on the sidewalks of open roads. If you can, pray it along with the movement of traffic. When you see green lights, weave that into your prayer — feel that forward momentum, declaring, "There are always green lights for me. The roads are open before me." Let the energy of moving cars, buses, and bicycles inspire your own spiritual motion.

If you come to a red light, you can choose to make a right or left turn and keep following the green lights. Think of it as a prophetic act: the detour may represent the way God is taking you to your destination. Sometimes He'll give you a shortcut, sometimes the scenic route, but either way, the road is still open for you. Every step becomes a declaration of divine movement.

Road opening is rarely just about a door swinging open in front of you. Mary, the angels, and your spiritual allies will often clear the path through other people — a friend offering help, a stranger pointing you toward a new opportunity, or a contact introducing you to someone who changes everything.

The Bible reminds us that blessings and divine messages often arrive through unexpected sources. Many times, it wasn't the high priests or the most "religiously pure" individuals who carried God's messages —

it was those considered outsiders. Gentiles, the so-called "unclean," and those on the fringes of society were often the vessels for God's will. Even John the Baptist, living in the wilderness, was chosen to prepare the way for Jesus.

In the same way, your open road may be delivered by someone you least expect. Be open to Spirit's movement in every form, because the person you might overlook could be the very one carrying your key to breakthrough.

Opening Prayer

Blessed Mother Mary, Our Lady of the Way, I come before you seeking clarity, blessing, and the removal of all blockages in my path. By your intercession, may the road before me be cleared of harm, confusion, and delay, so that I may walk fully into God's purpose for my life. May every prayer bead I hold carry my faith, and every word I speak unlock the blessings of heaven. Amen.

First Decade – God Makes a Way in the Wilderness

"I will make a way in the wilderness and rivers in the desert." – **Isaiah 43:19**

Meditation: God's ability to open roads is not dependent on human logic; He creates paths where none exist.

Reflection: What places in my life feel like deserts? Can I trust God to bring life and a way forward even here?

Affirmation: God is making a clear and beautiful path for me, even now.

Hoodoo Correspondences: Psalm 23 ("He leads me beside still waters...") Candle Color: Orange (road opening, attraction) Herb: Lemongrass (clearing blockages, drawing blessings) Working Idea: Place lemongrass at the base of an orange candle, pray Psalm 23 while holding your rosary, then begin the decade.

Second Decade – The Exodus Pathway

"The Lord will fight for you; you need only to be still."
– Exodus 14:14

Meditation: God parted the Red Sea for His people to walk in freedom; He can part any "sea" in your life.

Reflection: What "sea" or impossible situation do I need God to part right now?

Affirmation: I walk forward in faith; my path is opened by God's own hand.

Hoodoo Correspondences: Psalm 114 (celebrating God's deliverance) Candle Color: Blue (peaceful passage, safe travel) Herb: Bay leaf (victory, divine favor) Working Idea: Write your goal or desired open road on a bay leaf; hold it while praying the decade, then place it under your candle.

Third Decade – Jesus Sends Out the Seventy-Two

"The harvest is plentiful, but the workers are few... Go! I am sending you out like lambs among wolves." – **Luke 10:2-3**

Meditation: Jesus opens doors of opportunity and sends you exactly where you're meant to go.

Reflection: Where is God sending me now? How can I step into this mission without fear?

Affirmation: I am guided into fruitful and safe opportunities.

Hoodoo Correspondences:Psalm 121 (protection on journeys) Candle Color: Yellow (success, joy, opportunities) Herb: Road opener herb blend (lemongrass, abre camino, basil) Working Idea: Light a yellow candle dressed with road opener oil while praying this decade, visualizing your opportunities opening.

Fourth Decade – Paul's Prison Doors Open

"Suddenly there was such a violent earthquake that the foundations of the prison were shaken. At once all the prison doors flew open." – **Acts 16:26**

Meditation: No chain, no gate, no prison can keep you from the destiny God has for you.

Reflection: What prison (literal or symbolic) do I need to be freed from?

Affirmation: Every chain is broken; every gate swings open before me.

Hoodoo Correspondences: Psalm 124 (deliverance from danger) Candle Color: White (purity, fresh start) Herb: Eucalyptus (clearing, uncrossing) Working Idea: Place eucalyptus leaves on your altar; as you pray this decade, fan the air toward you with them to "pull in" freedom.

Fifth Decade – The Open Door No One Can Shut

"See, I have placed before you an open door that no one can shut." – **Revelation 3:8**

Meditation: God's opened doors are permanent; no human hand can close what He has destined for you.

Reflection: Am I walking with gratitude and boldness through the doors God has opened?

Affirmation: The way before me is open and secure in God's plan.

Hoodoo Correspondences: Psalm 84 (blessings in God's dwelling and path) Candle Color: Green (growth, prosperity) Herb: Basil (prosperity, success) Working Idea: Brew basil tea, sprinkle a little at your doorstep while praying this decade to invite ongoing blessings.

Closing Prayer

Mary, Mother of the Open Road, I thank you for walking with me through every turning, every crossing, and every new beginning. I receive the blessings of clear paths, open doors, and safe travels in all areas of my life. May every road I walk lead me closer to God's will and deeper into divine abundance. Amen.

Romantic Rosary

This rosary is for those who want a love that feels like the poetry of Song of Solomon — not just romance, but a love that is stable, wise, faithful, and blessed by God. The kind of love where there's deep respect and attraction, laughter and security, spiritual partnership and physical delight.

For me, this rosary isn't about desperate chasing or frantic spellcasting. It's about attuning yourself to the vibration of the love you want to live in — so that when it arrives, you're already standing in it, already prepared to receive it. In my own work, I've seen that praying with this kind of intention doesn't just bring someone in — it transforms you into the partner you're praying for.

Opening Prayer

Blessed Mother Mary, Queen of Love, and Saint Valentine, I come before you in purity of intention and beauty of spirit, seeking a love that mirrors divine union — faithful, gentle, passionate, and enduring. Holy Spirit, guide my heart to one who is my complement in every way, that we may walk together in purpose, joy, and blessing. Amen.

1st Decade — Love That Sees You Clearly

"You are altogether beautiful, my darling; there is no flaw in you." – **Song of Solomon 4:7**

Meditation: See yourself through the eyes of Divine Love. Imagine your future spouse seeing your inner and outer beauty and cherishing it.

Reflection: Are you ready to be loved without condition, without criticism?

Affirmation: I am beautiful inside and out, and I attract a partner who sees my full worth.

Hoodoo Correspondences: Psalm: 45 (marriage blessing) Candle Color: Pink Herbs/Roots: Rose petals, cinnamon, damiana Working Idea: Dress a pink candle with attraction oil and sprinkle rose petals at your altar.

2nd Decade — Love That Protects

"Many waters cannot quench love; rivers cannot sweep it away." – **Song of Solomon 8:7**

Meditation: Visualize your love weathering all storms, enduring through time.

Reflection: How do you nurture love so it grows stronger under pressure?

Affirmation: My relationship is unshakable and protected by God's hand.

Hoodoo Correspondences: Psalm: 91 (protection over the relationship) Candle Color: Red Herbs/Roots: Bay leaves, basil, clove Working Idea: Make a protective charm bag for your future union.

3rd Decade — Love That Provides and Builds

"She is clothed with strength and dignity; she can laugh at the days to come." – **Proverbs 31:25**

Meditation: Imagine a relationship where both partners build a life of abundance and stability.

Reflection: Are you cultivating the traits of a partner who builds rather than drains?

Affirmation: My partner and I build a home of joy, prosperity, and love.

Hoodoo Correspondences:Psalm: 128 (prosperity and family blessing) Candle Color: Green Herbs/Roots: Alfalfa, cinnamon, patchouli Working Idea: Place alfalfa and cinnamon under your bed to draw prosperity with love.

4th Decade — Love That Delights

"I have found the one my soul loves." – **Song of Solomon 3:4**

Meditation: See the joy and playfulness in your love, the fun you share together.

Reflection: How do you keep joy and delight alive in a long-term union?

Affirmation: My love is filled with joy, laughter, and tender moments.

Hoodoo Correspondences: Psalm: 37:4 (delight in the Lord, desires fulfilled) Candle Color: Yellow Herbs/Roots: Orange peel, vanilla, catnip Working Idea: Burn a yellow candle with catnip sprinkled around it for joy and attraction.

5th Decade — Love That Honors God

"Two are better than one, because they have a good return for their labor." – **Ecclesiastes 4:9**

Meditation: Visualize you and your beloved walking together in faith and shared purpose.

Reflection: How will you keep God at the center of your love?

Affirmation: My love honors God and grows stronger in His presence.

Hoodoo Correspondences: Psalm: 23 (divine guidance and blessing) Candle Color: White Herbs/Roots: Frankincense, myrrh, lavender Working Idea: Burn frankincense and myrrh during prayer for spiritual blessing over your love.

Closing Prayer

Lord, I thank You for the promise of a love that is true, steadfast, and divinely appointed. May this relationship honor You, bring joy to our lives, and be a blessing to those around us. Mother Mary, guide me in purity, patience, and discernment. Amen.

Uncrossing Rosary

In my years as a working psychic and medium, I've done countless readings for people wanting to know exactly who was "working against them" and exactly how to remove it. But here's what I've learned: most of the time, no one is actually hexing them.

In the world of uncrossing work, we often rush to blame an outside source — a jealous friend, an angry ex, a hidden enemy — when the truth is far less dramatic but far more within our control. Many people don't realize that they are often the ones doing the crossing on themselves through repeated patterns, poor boundaries, and ignoring divine warnings.

Sometimes the "cross" in your life is:

- Staying in a relationship you know is toxic.

- Refusing to hold boundaries with family members who drain you.

- Filling your mind with music, media, or environments that keep you spiritually heavy.

- Avoiding the fast or prayer you know you've been called to do.

These aren't curses lit by someone else's candle — they're the natural consequences of moving against God's guidance for your life. And sometimes, bad luck is just divine redirection — a holy warning that you're headed down the wrong path.

That's why discernment is everything. Before you light a candle or pray this Uncrossing Rosary, pause and ask:

- Is this truly a spiritual attack?

- Or is this God showing me where I need to change course?

Praying this rosary is powerful — it clears what is spiritual in nature and strengthens you to walk free. But lasting freedom also comes from accountability, obedience, and aligning your daily choices with the path you know Heaven is calling you to walk.

Opening Prayer

Holy Mother Mary, Undoer of Knots, Mother of Mercy, I come to you with the chains of oppression, confusion, and blockage upon me. I ask you to walk with me through this prayer, undoing every knot, reversing every curse, and restoring my steps to the path God intended. By the authority of Jesus Christ, the covering of your mantle, and the power of the Holy Spirit, I declare that every dark work against me is now null and void. Amen.

First Decade – Psalm 37:12-15

"The wicked plot against the righteous and gnash their teeth at them; but the Lord laughs at the wicked, for He knows their day is coming. The swords of the wicked will pierce their own hearts, and their bows will be broken."

Meditation: See yourself surrounded by shields impenetrable by the swords and bows cast by your enemies.

Reflection: Have you been afraid of what others have said or done against you? Can you trust that God's justice is already unfolding, even if you can't yet see it?

Affirmation: "No weapon formed against me shall prosper. The works of my enemies fall back upon themselves."

Hoodoo Correspondences: Psalm: 37 Candle Color: White (purification, clarity) Herb: Hyssop (for spiritual cleansing) Working Idea: Pray this decade while bathing with hyssop and reciting Psalm 51 afterward.

Second Decade – Isaiah 54:17

"No weapon formed against you will prevail, and you will refute every tongue that accuses you. This is the heritage of the servants of the Lord."

Meditation: Your protection is your inheritance. As a child of God, no curse, hex, or slander can stick to you. You walk in spiritual authority, able to break every spoken or written word meant for harm. Imagine a child version of you playfully saying " I'm rubber and you're glue, whatever you say bounces off me and sticks to you!"

Reflection: Where have you allowed fear to give power to a curse? Can you reclaim your spiritual authority and speak back against the darkness?

Affirmation: "Every curse sent my way is broken now in the name of Jesus. I am free, clean, and whole."

Hoodoo Correspondences: Psalm: 91 Candle Color: Purple (authority, mastery) Herb: Rue (protection, breaking hexes) Working Idea: Light a purple candle dressed with rue oil and pray this decade over it daily until the condition breaks.

Third Decade – Psalm 51:7

"Cleanse me with hyssop, and I will be clean; wash me, and I will be whiter than snow."

Meditation: See yourself bright like a flame that no moth can touch.

Reflection: What spiritual dirt have you allowed to linger? Where can you invite God's cleansing to bring you into full renewal?

Affirmation: "I am washed clean in the name of Jesus. Every impurity, seen and unseen, leaves me now."

Hoodoo Correspondences: Psalm: 51 Candle Color: Blue (peace, healing) Herb: Hyssop (purification) Working Idea: Take a hyssop bath and air-dry while reciting this decade, envisioning every crossing being washed away.

Fourth Decade – Acts 16:26

"Suddenly there was such a violent earthquake that the foundations of the prison were shaken. At once all the prison doors flew open, and everyone's chains came loose."

Meditation: The same power that opened prison doors for Paul and Silas can shake loose any spiritual chains binding you. Your captivity — whether mental, emotional, or spiritual — cannot withstand God's freedom.

Reflection: What chains have you been carrying that aren't yours to carry? Can you envision the moment those locks break open?

Affirmation: "Every chain binding me is broken now. I walk free, unbound, and unstoppable."

Hoodoo Correspondences: Psalm: 124 Candle Color: Orange (road opening after uncrossing) Herb: Lemongrass (clearing away obstacles) Working Idea: Burn an orange candle anointed with lemongrass oil while praying this decade to push forward after uncrossing.

Fifth Decade – Luke 13:12-13

"When Jesus saw her, He called her forward and said, 'Woman, you are set free from your infirmity.' Then He put His hands on her, and immediately she straightened up and praised God."

Meditation: Imagine and feel yourself free from any affliction or worry of harm. See yourself joyously smiling.

Reflection: Are you ready to stand tall in your power again? Can you thank God now for the freedom you are stepping into?

Affirmation: "I am loosed from all bondage. I stand tall in victory."

Hoodoo Correspondences: Psalm: 23 Candle Color: Gold (victory, success) Herb: Bay leaves (victory, triumph) Working Idea: Write your name on a bay leaf, hold it while praying this decade, and then burn it to seal your freedom.

Closing Prayer

Blessed Mother, I thank you for walking with me through this uncrossing. By your intercession and the power of Christ, I am loosed from every chain, shielded from every arrow, and cleansed from every stain. No curse can cling to me, no hex can hold me, and no crossing can stay. I stand now in my freedom, giving thanks to God who delivers me. Amen.

The Hoodoo Mysteries

One of the most freeing things about working the rosary in Hoodoo is that you don't have to pray all five decades every time. While a full five-decade rosary can feel like a spiritual marathon — building power with each prayer — there's no rule that says you can't take a single decade and work it like a single, potent charm. Sometimes, that's all the time you'll have, and sometimes, that's all the energy you'll need.

If you're on your lunch break, walking to the bus, or sitting in your car before an appointment, you can take up your rosary and pray one decade with a laser focus on your intention. This allows you to work the beads consistently even in the busiest seasons of life.

One Decade, One Focus

Here's how this can work:

Choose your intention. What's most pressing right now? Do you need to open the way for a new opportunity? Draw more clients? Sweeten a difficult relationship? Protect your home?

Pick your mystery or scripture. You can choose from the traditional mysteries (for example, the Visitation for making new friends, the Wedding at Cana for marital blessings) or from one of the Hoodoo Mysteries in the coming section.

Set your space, or pray where you are. In Hoodoo, location and symbolism matter — but so does practicality. Pray your decade at a crossroads, at your work desk, in your kitchen, or even while walking.

Keep your prayer tight and focused. Your intention should thread through each Hail Mary or affirmation.

Why One Decade Can Be Enough

In my own practice, I've seen that one well-prayed decade, said with clear mind and heart, can move mountains. Prayer is like any other working — it's not always about quantity, but about alignment, consistency, and faith.

Remember: when you're praying the rosary in a Hoodoo context, you're not just saying words — you're sending petitions into the spiritual world, calling on allies, and putting energy in motion. The spirits you work with don't measure your sincerity by the number of beads you cover, but by the truth in your voice and the steadfastness in your heart.

What's Next

The next section offers you a variety of Mysteries designed for specific Hoodoo intentions. Each one follows the structure you've already learned and include:

- Road-Opening Mystery – Clearing blockages, finding your path, attracting opportunities.

- Money-Drawing Mystery – Increasing income, attracting paying clients, building wealth.

- Sweetening Work Mystery – Healing relationships, drawing kindness and favor, softening hearts.

- Protection Mystery – Guarding your spirit, home, and loved ones from harm.

- Healing Mystery – Physical recovery, emotional wholeness, spiritual renewal.

You can use these Mysteries for a quick, potent boost toward your goal or to simply contemplate upon different verses within the Bible.

Road Opening Mystery

"I will go before thee, and make the crooked places straight: I will break in pieces the gates of brass, and cut in sunder the bars of iron." — **Isaiah 45:2**

Meditation: See Mary walking ahead of you, gently unlocking each door, sweeping obstacles aside with her mantle, and clearing your path with holy light.

Reflection: What doors have I been afraid to knock on, and how can I trust Spirit to open them for me?

Affirmation: "Every door that is meant for me is opening now, and nothing can block my way."

Money Drawing Mystery

"Wealth and riches shall be in his house: and his righteousness endureth for ever."— **Psalm 112:3**

Meditation: Imagine your home filled with abundance — food on the table, bills paid, savings growing — all blessed and protected under Mary's care.

Reflection: How do I define prosperity, and am I open to receiving it in new and unexpected ways?

Affirmation: "I welcome divine prosperity into my life with gratitude and integrity."

Physical Healing Mystery

"For I will restore health unto thee, and I will heal thee of thy wounds, saith the LORD." 7 — **Jeremiah 30:1**

Meditation: See Mary placing her hands over your body, or over the person you're praying for, filling every cell with golden light and renewed life.

Reflection: What part of me — body, mind, or spirit — is calling for healing today?

Affirmation: "I am whole, I am restored, I am in harmony with divine health."

Protection Mystery

"For he shall give his angels charge over thee, to keep thee in all thy ways." — **Psalm 91:11**

Meditation: Picture Mary wrapping her mantle around you like a fortress, while angels stand guard at every direction — north, south, east, and west.

Reflection: Where do I need to set stronger spiritual or physical boundaries in my life?

Affirmation: "I am divinely shielded; no curse, hex, or ill will can touch me."

Love Drawing Mystery

"I found him whom my soul loveth: I held him, and would not let him go." — **Song of Solomon 3:4**

Meditation: Imagine Mary introducing you to the person, community, or opportunity that will love and honor you, and feel that love expand from your heart outward.

Reflection: Am I ready to receive love in the form that is truly good for me, even if it looks different from what I expected?

Affirmation: "I attract and nurture love that is aligned, mutual, and blessed."

Justice Mystery

"But let judgment run down as waters, and righteousness as a mighty stream." — **Amos 5:24**

Affirmation: "Divine justice flows into every situation of my life, setting all things right."

Meditation: See Mary pouring out a pitcher of pure, clear water over a situation of injustice, washing away lies, corruption, and imbalance.

Reflection: Where do I need to trust God's timing for justice, and where am I being called to act?

Ancestor Gateway Mystery

"Wherefore seeing we also are compassed about with so great a cloud of witnesses, let us lay aside every weight." — **Hebrews 12:1**

Affirmation: "I am guided, protected, and blessed by my righteous ancestors."

Meditation: Picture Mary standing at a gate, surrounded by your ancestors in light, each smiling and placing blessings in your hands for the road ahead.

Reflection: What wisdom from my ancestors is ready to come through to me now, and how will I honor it?

Sweetening Work Mystery

"Pleasant words are as a honeycomb, sweet to the soul, and health to the bones." — **Proverbs 16:24**

Affirmation: "My words and presence are sweet, drawing kindness, favor, and goodwill."

Meditation: See Mary pouring golden honey over the situation or person you wish to soften, until it is surrounded in sweetness and peace.

Reflection: Where could a softer approach open more doors for me?

Court Case Favor Mystery

"Plead my cause, O LORD, with them that strive with me: fight against them that fight against me." — **Psalm 35:1**

Affirmation: "Divine justice is on my side; truth and fairness prevail."

Meditation: Picture Mary standing beside you in the courtroom, whispering truth into the ears of all decision-makers.

Reflection: Am I willing to let go of revenge so that divine justice can flow unhindered?

Blessed Mystery

"Bless the LORD, O my soul... Who healeth all thy diseases." — **Psalm 103:2-3**

Meditation: Imagine Mary pouring oil of light over your head, flowing through your entire body, bringing health and renewal.

Reflection: Where can I speak blessings over myself and others more consistently?

Affirmation: "I am blessed and restored; healing flows through me now."

Breaking Hexes Mystery

"No weapon that is formed against thee shall prosper." — **Isaiah 54:17**

Meditation: See Mary cutting cords of darkness with a golden sword, scattering all harmful works back to the void.

Reflection: What habits or connections do I need to release to stay spiritually clear?

Affirmation: "Every chain is broken; every curse is undone in the power of God."

Prophetic Dreams & Visions Mystery

"Your old men shall dream dreams, your young men shall see visions." — **Joel 2:28**

Meditation: Picture Mary placing a veil of silver light over your head as you sleep, opening your inner sight to holy messages.

Reflection: How will I record and honor the messages I receive in dreams?

Affirmation: "I am open to divine messages through dreams and visions."

The Walking Rosary: Protection in Motion

One of my favorite methods of layering the rosary into a working is the rosary walk. If you want to protect your home, walk the perimeter of your property or your block while praying the rosary. You can use a small one-decade rosary that fits in your pocket, making it discreet. In urban settings, wearing headphones can make it appear as though you're simply on a call.

You can pray aloud if comfortable, or silently if you prefer. The effect is the same — each bead a spiritual bell ringing through the air. This practice echoes the tradition of Celtic monks, who would chant psalms as they worked and walked, saturating the land with prayer.

Rosary walks turn your entire neighborhood into a consecrated space, charged bead by bead, step by step.

15

What You Can Expect from the Hoodoo Rosary Path

When you commit to praying the rosary — and especially when you bring it into your Hoodoo practice — you are stepping into a living stream of prayer that has been flowing for centuries.

This is not just about words repeated over beads. This is about forming a relationship with Mary, with the Divine, and with the great cloud of witnesses that surrounds you — your ancestors, the angels, the saints, and the holy ones who walk unseen at your side.

With time and devotion, here's what often unfolds:

- A deepened connection to your ancestors — especially your Christian ancestors, whose faith and prayers shaped the path you stand on today.

- An expansion of your spiritual allies — angels, saints, and biblical figures may begin to make themselves known to you in dreams, signs, and sudden inspirations.

- A new way of seeing scripture — where Bible verses become mystical keys, and the mysteries of the rosary open into truths about manifestation, astrology, numerology, and the timeless wisdom found across faith traditions.

- An inner strengthening — in discernment, in protection, in clarity about who you are and the power you carry.

- A change in your life without forcing it — doors begin to open, obstacles move, and blessings arrive, often without you even needing to ask.

- A stronger willpower — you will find yourself more easily saying no to vices and temptations.

- A pull towards all things holy — you will find yourself removing activities and behaviors from your life that do not serve you and replacing them with healthier, holier alternatives. For example, you will have a propensity towards cleansing your body with clean foods, your soul with prayer and spiritual exercises, and your community with your gifts or alms.

- Stronger magical abilities — your ability to focus and invision will be finetuned from using it in the rosary so that you can use this skill in your other magical workings.

- Psychopomp and more intense spiritual workings — you may find yourself intercessing on behalf of others.

In the following sections, I share some of the most profound transformations I've experienced from walking this path — and how you may experience them too.

Coming Home to My Christian Ancestors

I never had hurt toward Christianity. For me, it wasn't about rejecting the faith entirely — it was more that I thought it would be cooler to not be associated with Christianity at all. I didn't want the label of "Christian," much less "Christian witch." I wanted to just be a witch. I wanted to stand in my magic without that label following me.

But through working with my ancestors, I learned that it's totally fine — in fact, deeply powerful — to have Christian tied to my magic. I began to see how much of my magic and my spiritual resilience comes directly from my Christian ancestry.

And something shifted: I began to love Mary, the angels and the traditional Christian icons and paraphernalia. I realized that embracing my Christian ancestors did not mean embracing hypocrisy or judgmental religion. It meant reclaiming the beauty and spiritual fire that my ancestors carried — even if modern-day Pharisees and Sadducees would never understand it.

For You:

As you walk this Hoodoo Rosary path, you might find yourself softening toward the label "Christian" or "Catholic." You may start to see the cross, the rosary, and Mary not as symbols of restriction, but as living spiritual allies. And if you have initial resistance — that's natural. Many of us don't want to be associated with those who claim Christ but show no love. This practice will help you see past the noise and connect to the living truth.

Walking with Angels and Saints

Before I started praying the rosary, Archangel Michael was already in my life. He had come to me while I was working as a medium, and I loved his strong, protective presence. But praying the rosary deepened that connection beyond anything I expected. Now, I don't just feel Michael beside me — I feel his protection wrapped around me like a shield. I see him and signs of his presence everywhere.

I've also begun to grow closer to Saint Anne, feeling her grandmotherly guidance and care, and my awareness of the angels has expanded. Praying the rosary has given me clearer discernment — not just in spiritual matters, but in everyday choices. I find myself more often than not, in the right place at the right time, as if heaven is gently steering me.

For You:

As you devote yourself to the rosary, you may find angels and saints quietly stepping forward in your life. You may have vivid dreams, feel nudges of inspiration, or develop a sudden interest in a saint you've never thought about before. Welcome these relationships. They will walk beside you, guide you, and help you carry your work with more power and grace. * <u>Keep in mind that not all saints are recognized by the church. A saint is any being who has exhibited an exceptional holiness and closeness to God, led a virtuous life, offered their life for others, or were martyred for their faith.</u>

Seeing the Mysteries Unfold

The more I pray the rosary, the more I see the Bible differently. I'm beginning to read it daily — not out of obligation, but because each page now feels alive with layers of meaning. I'm seeing the mysticism behind the stories, how the Bible contains keys to manifestation, and how its mysteries mirror the mythologies of other lands and times.

I see echoes of Isis, of ancient goddesses, in the figure of Mary. I see the threads of astrology and numerology woven through the text. The rosary has become a way for me to unlock these connections, to stand in awe of how vast and interconnected spiritual truth really is.

For You:

As you continue on this path, expect your spiritual sight to sharpen. You may start to notice patterns between the Bible and other sacred traditions you study. You may receive insight into the mysteries of scripture that changes how you pray, how you work magic, and how you see your own life story. The rosary is not the end of this journey — it's the beginning of a much deeper unfolding.

Night Work, Dreams, and the Psychopomp Path

Another fruit of the Hoodoo Rosary is what I call night work. As you deepen in this practice, you may find that your prayers spill over into your dream life, that the beads mark you not only in waking but in sleep.

I myself have had many nights where I wake knowing I have been praying the rosary all night long. At times I've found myself interceding for others, even those I don't know — carrying them in prayer during times of illness, fear, or transition. In dreams I have stood beside souls as they crossed over, present in the holy work of being a guide and comforter at the hour of death. The rosary has made me a psychopomp, not by ritual choice, but by grace.

I have heard the voice of God in dreams — unmistakable, powerful, loving, and commanding. I have also seen Archangel Michael in vivid dreams, and even outside of dreams as a direct result of my rosary practice. His presence is not just something I "feel" — I have seen him, more strongly and more clearly than ever before. I was already working with him as a medium before my rosary life began, but through the rosary my connection with him has deepened to an entirely new level.

There have also been dreams where I was surrounded by prayer — voices chanting the Ave Maria in Latin, filling entire dreamscapes with holiness. In those moments I realized I wasn't just dreaming — I was praying, and being prayed through.

You may find this happening to you as well. The rosary opens doors not only to mystical understanding but to mystical responsibility. You may become an intercessor without trying, one whose nightly prayers protect others. You may become a dreamer who works between the worlds. You may wake knowing that your prayers have moved, shielded, or released someone.

This may feel strange at first, but it is a gift. It means your rosary practice has become larger than yourself — it is alive, moving through you as a force of protection, guidance, and healing. And if your dreams become more vivid, if your nights become spiritually "busy," know that you are not alone. The angels, the saints, your ancestors, and the Virgin herself walk with you in that unseen night shift, and your prayers continue when your lips are still.

16

Living the Prayer

You've learned the prayers. You've explored the mysteries. You've prayed through intentions and walked with the saints, angels, Mary, and the ancestors. Now the rosary is no longer just a set of beads in your hand — it's a living cord that ties you to Heaven, Earth, and all who walk this path with you.

When I first began praying the rosary in this way, I didn't know where it would lead. I prayed in devotion, sometimes with petitions, sometimes without — and in time, the prayers began to change me. My connection with my ancestors deepened. My relationship with Mary became more intimate. I could feel the protection of the angels not just during ritual, but in my everyday life. I began to notice that the rosary wasn't something I "picked up" anymore. It was something I carried inside of me, every hour of the day.

And that is the gift I want you to take with you: the knowing that this path will grow with you.

You will change.

Your prayers will change.

Your relationship with the Divine will shift and expand.

The Ongoing Path

The rosary doesn't end when you set it down. It will continue to work within you, opening roads, closing harmful doors, deepening your discernment, and connecting you more strongly to the spirits and holy ones who walk beside you.

Keep a journal. Pay attention to dreams. Notice the ways answers arrive — sometimes in direct, miraculous bursts, and sometimes in the quiet unfolding of daily life. Try seasons of devotion: a 9-day novena, a 30-day immersion, or a 54-day journey. Return to the mysteries again and again; each visit will reveal something new.

Becoming a Prayer

The more you pray, the more you become the prayer. People may begin to sense something different about you — a peace, a quiet authority, a blessing you carry without speaking. Your words will carry more weight. Your presence will soothe, heal, and inspire.

You may not notice it at first, but others will. This is the natural fruit of devotion.

Passing the Flame

Hoodoo has always been a tradition of passing on what works, sharing what blesses, and teaching the next person how to survive and thrive.

This rosary is no different.

Share it with your children, friends, community — whoever is ready to receive it. You don't have to explain everything at once. Sometimes the beads will do the teaching for you.

Closing Benediction

May Mary, the angels, and your ancestors guide you through life's mysteries.

The Traditional Mysteries with Scripture

The Joyful Mysteries

1. The Annunciation

"Behold, I am the handmaid of the Lord; let it be to me according to your word."(Luke 1:26-38)

Reflection: Reflect on Mary's "yes" to God's plan.

2. The Visitation

"Blessed are you among women, and blessed is the fruit of your womb!"(Luke 1:39-56)

Reflection: Consider the joy of sharing God's blessings with others and being able to be of service.

3. The Nativity

"And she gave birth to her firstborn son and wrapped him in swaddling cloths and laid him in a manger."(Luke 2:1-20)

Reflection: Meditate on the humility of Christ's birth and the gift of God's presence in our lives.

4. The Presentation in the Temple

"My eyes have seen your salvation."(Luke 2:22-38)

Reflection: Reflect on the act of offering your life and loved ones to God, trusting in His plan.

5. The Finding of Jesus in the Temple

"Did you not know that I must be in my Father's house?" (Luke 2:41-50)

Reflection: Pray for the wisdom to seek God in all things and to trust in His timing.

Sorrowful Mysteries

1. The Agony in the Garden

"Father, if you are willing, take this cup from me; yet not my will, but yours be done." (Luke 22:42)

Reflection: Reflect on the moments of trial in your life, asking for the grace to surrender to God's divine will, even in times of suffering and uncertainty.

2. The Scourging at the Pillar

"Then Pilate took Jesus and had Him flogged." (John 19:1)

Reflection: Meditate on Christ's suffering and sacrifice, offering up your own pain in union with His for the redemption of the world.

3. The Crowning with Thorns

"They clothed Him in a purple robe and went up to Him again and again, saying, 'Hail, king of the Jews!' And they slapped Him in the face." (John 19:2-3)

Reflection: Consider the humiliation and mockery Christ endured, and invite God to help you cultivate humility and patience in the face of adversity.

4. The Carrying of the Cross

"Whoever wants to be my disciple must deny themselves and take up their cross daily and follow me." (Luke 9:23)

Reflection: Reflect on your personal crosses and how you can carry them with love and perseverance, trusting in God's strength to help you.

5. The Crucifixion and Death of Jesus

"Father, into your hands I commit my spirit." (Luke 23:46)

Reflection: Contemplate the depth of Christ's love for humanity and His ultimate sacrifice. Offer yourself fully to God's plan, letting go of what holds you back.

Glorious Mysteries

1. The Resurrection

"He is not here; He has risen, just as He said." (Matthew 28:6)

Reflection: Rejoice in the victory of Christ over death and find renewed hope and faith in His promise of eternal life.

2. The Ascension

"He was taken up before their very eyes, and a cloud hid Him from their sight." (Acts 1:9)

Reflection: Reflect on Christ's ascension as a call to set your heart on heavenly things and trust that He is always with you.

3. The Descent of the Holy Spirit

"They saw what seemed to be tongues of fire that separated and came to rest on each of them. All of them were filled with the Holy Spirit." (Acts 2:3-4)

Reflection: Reflect on the gift of the Holy Spirit, who empowers and guides us to live out our faith boldly and with love.

4. The Assumption of Mary

"The queen stands at your right hand, arrayed in gold." (Psalm 45:9)

Reflection: Consider Mary's assumption into heaven as a reminder of the promise of eternal life for those who live faithfully.

5. The Coronation of Mary

"A great sign appeared in heaven: a woman clothed with the sun, with the moon under her feet and a crown of twelve stars on her head." (Revelation 12:1)

Reflection: Reflect on Mary's coronation as Queen of Heaven and Earth, symbolizing the fulfillment of God's promises and the glory awaiting the faithful.

Luminous Mysteries

1. The Baptism of Jesus in the Jordan

"And when Jesus was baptized, immediately he went up from the water, and behold, the heavens were opened to him." (Matthew 3:16)

Reflection: Jesus' baptism invites us to renew our own baptismal promises and recognize our identity as beloved children of God.

2. The Wedding at Cana

"His mother said to the servants, 'Do whatever he tells you.'" (John 2:5)

Reflection: The transformation of water into wine at Cana reminds us of God's abundant blessings and the trust we should place in His will.

3. The Proclamation of the Kingdom

"Jesus went throughout Galilee, teaching in their synagogues, proclaiming the good news of the kingdom, and healing every disease and sickness among the people."(Matthew 4:23)

Reflection: Through His proclamation of the Kingdom, Jesus invites us to repentance, renewal, and a deeper relationship with God. His words and miracles remind us of the hope and joy found in living according to the Gospel.

4. The Transfiguration

"As he was praying, the appearance of his face changed, and his clothes became as bright as a flash of lightning." (Luke 9:29)

Reflection: The Transfiguration reveals Jesus in His divine glory, strengthening the faith of His disciples and offering a glimpse of the eternal life promised to us. It is a moment of awe that calls us to listen to and follow Him wholeheartedly.

5. The Institution of the Eucharist

"Then he took a cup, and when he had given thanks, he gave it to them, saying, 'Drink from it, all of you. This is my blood of the covenant, which is poured out for many for the forgiveness of sins.'" (Matthew 26:27-28)

Reflection: The institution of the Eucharist is the ultimate gift of Christ's love, offering His very body and blood for the salvation of humanity. It reminds us of the depth of His sacrifice and calls us to unity with Him and one another.

The Seven Joys of Mary Rosary

The Seven Joys of Mary

The Seven Joys Rosary, or Franciscan Crown, celebrates joyful events in Mary's life and originated with the Franciscans in the 15th century. Its history traces back to a young Franciscan novice who honored Mary by offering flowers to her statue. Mary appeared to him, suggesting he honor her joys through prayer instead. Inspired, he structured a rosary around seven key moments of joy in Mary's life, creating the Franciscan Crown Rosary, a rosary with seven decades.

1. The Annunciation

"The angel Gabriel was sent from God to a town of Galilee called Nazareth, to a virgin betrothed to a man named Joseph."(Luke 1:26-38)

Reflection: Mary's "yes" to God's plan reminds us of the power of surrender and trust in divine will.

2. The Visitation

"When Elizabeth heard Mary's greeting, the infant leaped in her womb, and Elizabeth, filled with the Holy Spirit, cried out in a loud voice." (Luke 1:39-56)

Reflection: The bond between Mary and Elizabeth shows the beauty of spiritual community and shared joy.

3. The Nativity

"And she gave birth to her firstborn son. She wrapped him in swaddling clothes and laid him in a manger."(Luke 2:1-20)

Reflection: Jesus' humble birth in a stable teaches us that greatness is often found in simplicity.

4. The Adoration of the Magi

"They were overjoyed at seeing the star, and on entering the house, they saw the child with Mary, his mother."(Matthew 2:1-12)

Reflection: The Magi's journey reminds us to seek truth and adore God's presence in our lives.

5. The Finding of Jesus in the Temple

"After three days they found him in the temple, sitting in the midst of the teachers, listening to them and asking them questions." (Luke 2:41-50)

Reflection: Even in moments of confusion, Jesus shows us the importance of being in our Father's house.

6. The Resurrection

"Why do you seek the living among the dead? He is not here, but he has been raised." (Luke 24:1-12)

Reflection: The Resurrection offers hope and renewal, reminding us of the victory over sin and death.

7. The Assumption and Coronation of Mary

(No direct scripture reference, though it is rooted in sacred tradition.)

Reflection: Mary's Assumption inspires us to look toward heaven and trust in God's promise of eternal life.

Promises of the 7 Joys of Mary Rosary

Devotion to the 7 Joys of Mary Rosary, also known as the Franciscan Crown Rosary, is accompanied by profound promises and spiritual graces. Those who recite this rosary with genuine faith and devotion can expect a deepening of their relationship with the Blessed Virgin Mary and an increased awareness of her intercessory power.

Specific indulgences have been granted by the Church for its recitation, particularly by friars of the Franciscan Order and the faithful who honor Mary's joys. Graces include consolation in times of distress, growth in humility, and the strengthening of faith and hope in God's promises.

The Seven Sorrows of Mary Rosary

The Seven Sorrows Rosary, also known as the Servite Rosary, focuses on the sorrowful events in Mary's life. It was popularized by the Servite Order in the 13th century and is prayed on a special rosary with seven sets of seven beads.

1. The Prophecy of Simeon

"Behold, this child is appointed for the fall and rising of many in Israel, and for a sign that is opposed (and a sword will pierce through your own soul also), so that thoughts from many hearts may be revealed." (Luke 2:34-35)

Reflection: Pray for the grace to accept God's will, even when it brings sorrow.

2. The Flight into Egypt

"Rise, take the child and his mother, and flee to Egypt, and remain there until I tell you, for Herod is about to search for the child, to destroy him." (Matthew 2:13)

Reflection: Reflect on Mary's trust in God's protection during times of uncertainty.

3. The Loss of the Child Jesus in the Temple

"After three days they found him in the temple, sitting among the teachers, listening to them and asking them questions." (Luke 2:46)

Reflection: Pray for the grace to seek God when He feels distant.

4. Mary Meets Jesus on the Way to Calvary

"And there followed him a great multitude of the people and of women who were mourning and lamenting for him." (Luke 23:27)

Reflection: Reflect on Mary's strength and pray for the courage to accompany others in their suffering.

5. The Crucifixion and Death of Jesus

"When Jesus saw his mother and the disciple whom he loved standing nearby, he said to his mother, 'Woman, behold, your son!'" (John 19:26)

Reflection: Meditate on Mary's sorrow at the foot of the cross and pray for the grace to unite your suffering with Christ's.

6. The Body of Jesus is Taken Down from the Cross

"Then he took it down and wrapped it in a linen shroud and laid him in a tomb cut in stone, where no one had ever yet been laid." (Luke 23:53)

Reflection: Pray for the grace to find peace in moments of loss.

7. The Burial of Jesus

"The women who had come with him from Galilee followed and saw the tomb and how his body was laid. Then they returned and prepared spices and ointments." (Luke 23:55-56)

Reflection: Reflect on Mary's hope in the resurrection and pray for the grace to trust in God's promises.

Promises of the Seven Sorrows Rosary

Those who have a devotion to the Seven Sorrows Rosary are promised seven special graces, as revealed by the Blessed Virgin Mary:

1. I will bring peace to their families.

2. They will gain an understanding of divine mysteries.

3. I will comfort them in their sufferings and support them in their work.

4. I will grant them what they ask for, as long as it aligns with the will of my divine Son and the sanctification of their souls.

5. I will protect them in spiritual battles against the infernal enemy and guard them throughout their lives.

6. I will assist them visibly at the hour of their death, allowing them to see the face of their Mother.

7. I have obtained from my divine Son the grace that those who spread this devotion to my tears and sorrows will pass directly from this earthly life to eternal happiness, with all their sins forgiven, and my Son and I will be their everlasting comfort and joy.

The Psalms and the Mysteries

In Hoodoo, the psalms are more than scripture — they are spells, incantations, and formulas of power. Historians recognize the psalms as some of the oldest writings in the Bible, often described as a spellbook filled with rituals and potent verses. Some even cite Psalm 109 as one of the oldest known curses, showcasing the psalms' deep ties to magical practices. These writings are believed by some to predate Christianity, linking the African Diaspora to even older streams of magic and spiritual traditions.

The structure of the psalms is inherently magical. Many like Psalm 27 follow a pattern of praise, petition, and declaration — a formula found in spellcraft across cultures. In this way, a psalm not only calls upon God, but stirs the God-power within the one praying. The psalms invite divine presence, ignite faith, and remind the soul of its own creative authority.

Within the Book of Psalms, you can find a remedy for almost anything:

- Love and reconciliation

- Protection from enemies
- Justice in court cases
- Prosperity and open roads
- Healing for body and spirit

For generations, our ancestors turned to the psalms as both prayer and conjure formula. They spoke them over floor washes, into healing teas, during candle burnings, and over charms. Each psalm carried a vibration that could shift the energy of a situation.

When you bring the psalms into the Hoodoo Rosary, you unlock a layered form of working. The mysteries of the rosary provide the imagery and meditation focus. The psalm provides the spoken spell. Together, they direct the flow of energy bead by bead.

You can pair an associated psalm with a particular decade and carry its power through your meditation, using that decade as a focused container for magical work. For example:

- Money Drawing: Pray Psalm 65 ("Praise waiteth for thee, O God, in Sion...") alongside the Joyful Mystery of the Visitation, envisioning blessings arriving swiftly, just as Mary brought grace to Elizabeth's household.

- Protection: Pray Psalm 91 with the Glorious Mystery of the Coronation, seeing yourself crowned with divine safety and surrounded by angels.

- Healing: Pray Psalm 103 with the Luminous Mystery of the Baptism of Jesus, feeling the cleansing waters restore your strength.

In this way, every mystery can become a spell code, and every psalm can be a conjure formula. When prayed through the rosary, the psalm's vibration is braided with the imagery of the mystery and the intention of the worker — creating a complete act of devotion, meditation, and magic all at once.

Notes: Psalms for Hoodoo Intentions

Intention	Psalm(s)	Mystery	Conjure Use
Money Drawing & Prosperity	Psalm 65, Psalm 23	The Visitation (Joyful)	Swift arrival of blessings, abundance, and good news.
Protection from Enemies	Psalm 91, Psalm 35	The Coronation of Mary (Glorious)	Shields from harm, calls angelic defense, secures favor.
Healing & Restoration	Psalm 103, Psalm 30	The Baptism of Jesus (Luminous)	Restores vitality, purifies body and spirit.
Love Drawing & Reconciliation	Psalm 45, Psalm 121	The Wedding at Cana (Luminous)	Draws romance, restores harmony between lovers.
Justice & Court Case Favor	Psalm 35, Psalm 7	The Resurrection (Glorious)	Turns judgment in your favor, reveals truth.
Breaking Curses & Uncrossing	Psalm 37, Psalm 140	The Crucifixion (Sorrowful)	Breaks evil workings, removes crossed conditions.
Guidance & Wisdom	Psalm 25, Psalm 111	The Finding in the Temple (Joyful)	Brings clarity in decision-making, divine insight.
Success & Victory	Psalm 21, Psalm 84	The Ascension (Glorious)	Overcomes obstacles, crowns efforts with success.

Marian Feast Days

1. Annunciation – March 25

Celebrates the angel Gabriel's announcement to Mary that she would bear Jesus. Observed widely: Roman Catholic (as a solemnity), Orthodox (as one of the Great Feasts), Anglican, Lutheran, and others.

2. Nativity of the Blessed Virgin Mary – September 8

Honoring Mary's birth. Celebrated by Catholic, Orthodox, Syriac, and Anglican traditions.

3. Dormition (Orthodox) / Assumption (Catholic) – August 15

Eastern Orthodox & Oriental Orthodox: Called the Dormition, marking Mary's "falling asleep" followed by Assumption (ascending to heaven).

Catholic Church: Known as the Assumption, when Mary, body and soul, was assumed into heaven — formally defined as dogma in 1950.

4. Solemnity of Mary, Mother of God

Catholic: Celebrated on January 1 (Octave of Christmas).

Eastern (Byzantine, Syriac Rites): Celebrated on December 26.

Coptic Orthodox: Observed on January 16 .

Additional Marian Feast Days (Not Exhaustive)

Presentation (Purification) – February 2 (Candlemas) .

Visitation of Mary to Elizabeth – May 31 .

Día de la Virgen de los Ángeles – August 2 .

Our Lady of the Rosary – October 7 .

Our Lady of Guadalupe – December 12 .

Our Lady of Sorrows – September 15 .

Feast Days in Other Orthodox Traditions

Some Eastern rites celebrate additional feasts:

Syriac Orthodox

January 15 – Virgin Mary of the Sowing

May 15 – Virgin Mary of the Harvest

December 26 – Glorification of the Mother of God .

Malankara Orthodox

January 1, January 15, March 25, May 15, August 15, September 8, December 26 .

Ethiopian & Eritrean Orthodox (Filseta)

A two-week fast from August 7–22 commemorates the Dormition/Assumption of Mary; August 15 is the main day .

Popular Marian Prayers

Litany of the Blessed Virgin Mary

Lord, have mercy on us. *Christ, have mercy on us.*
Lord, have mercy on us. *Christ hear us. Christ, graciously hear us.*

God the Father of heaven, *Have mercy on us.*
God the Son, Redeemer of the world, *Have mercy on us.*
God the Holy Spirit, *Have mercy on us.*
Holy Trinity, one God, *Have mercy on us.*

Holy Mary, *Pray for us. (repeat after each line)*
Holy Mother of God,
Holy Virgin of virgins,
Mother of Christ,
Mother of the Church,
Mother of mercy,
Mother of divine grace,
Mother of hope,
Mother most pure,
Mother most chaste,
Mother inviolate,
Mother undefiled,
Mother most amiable,

Mother most admirable,
Mother of good counsel,
Mother of our Creator,
Mother of our Savior,
Virgin most prudent,
Virgin most venerable,
Virgin most renowned,
Virgin most powerful,
Virgin most merciful,
Virgin most faithful,
Mirror of justice,
Seat of wisdom,
Cause of our joy,
Spiritual vessel,
Vessel of honor,
Singular vessel of devotion,
Mystical rose,
Tower of David,
Tower of ivory,

House of gold,
Ark of the covenant,
Gate of heaven,
Morning star,
Health of the sick,
Refuge of sinners,
Comfort of Migrants,
Comforter of the afflicted,
Help of Christians,
Queen of Angels,

Queen of Patriarchs,
Queen of Prophets,
Queen of Apostles,
Queen of Martyrs,
Queen of Confessors,
Queen of Virgins,
Queen of all Saints,
Queen conceived without original sin,
Queen assumed into heaven,
Queen of the most holy Rosary,
Queen of Families,
Queen of Peace,

Lamb of God, you take away the sins of the world, *Spare us, O Lord.*
Lamb of God, you take away the sins of the world, *Graciously hear us, O Lord.*
Lamb of God, you take away the sins of the world, *Have mercy on us.*

Pray for us, O holy Mother of God, *That we may be made worthy of the promises of Christ.*

Let us pray, Grant, we beseech you, Lord God, that we your servants may rejoice in continual health of mind and body and, by the glorious intercession of Blessed Mary, ever Virgin, may we be delivered from present sorrow to delight in joy eternal. Through Christ our Lord. Amen.

The Prayer of Mary (The Magnificat)

My soul proclaims the greatness of the Lord,
my spirit rejoices in God my Savior
for he has looked with favor on his lowly servant.
From this day all generations will call me blessed:
the Almighty has done great things for me,
and holy is his Name.

He has mercy on those who fear him
in every generation.
He has shown the strength of his arm,
he has scattered the proud in their conceit.

He has cast down the mighty from their thrones,
and has lifted up the lowly.
He has filled the hungry with good things,
and the rich he has sent away empty.

He has come to the help of his servant Israel
for he remembered his promise of mercy,
the promise he made to our fathers,
to Abraham and his children forever.

Memorare

Remember, O most gracious Virgin Mary, that never was it known that anyone who fled to thy protection, implored thy help, or sought thine intercession was left unaided.

Inspired by this confidence, I fly unto thee, O Virgin of virgins, my mother; to thee do I come, before thee I stand, sinful and sorrowful. O Mother of the Word Incarnate, despise not my petitions, but in thy mercy hear and answer me.

Amen.

Marian Titles

Litany of Loreto — Core Invocations

These are the traditional titles and invocations used in the Litany of the Blessed Virgin Mary, representing her virtues and roles :

- Holy Mother of God

- Holy Virgin of Virgins

- Mother of Christ

- Mother of the Church

- Mother of Mercy

- Mother of Divine Grace

- Mother of Hope

- Mother Most Pure / Chaste / Inviolate / Undefiled

- Mother Most Amiable / Admirable / of Good Counsel

- Mother of our Creator / Savior

- Virgin Most Prudent / Venerable / Renowned / Powerful / Merciful / Faithful

- Mirror of Justice

- Seat of Wisdom

- Cause of our Joy

- Spiritual Vessel / Vessel of Honor / Singlular Vessel of Devotion

- Mystical Rose

- Tower of David / Tower of Ivory

- House of Gold

- Ark of the Covenant

- Gate of Heaven

- Morning Star

- Health of the Sick

- Refuge of Sinners

- Solace of Migrants *(added June 2020)*

- Comfort of the Afflicted

- Help of Christians

- Queen of Angels / Patriarchs / Prophets / Apostles / Martyrs / Confessors / Virgins / All Saints

- Queen Conceived Without Original Sin / Assumed into Heaven / of the Most Holy Rosary / of Families / of Peace

Early & Theological Titles

These honor Mary's nature, role, and theological context :

- Our Lady / Blessed Virgin Mary (Madonna / Nuestra Señora / Notre Dame)

- Theotokos / Mother of God (Eastern tradition)

- Ever-Virgin, Spouse of the Holy Spirit

- Immaculate Conception — Our Lady of the Immaculate Conception

- Assumption — Queen Assumed into Heaven

- New Eve, Cause of Our Salvation

Popular Devotional Titles (Worldwide)

These titles are often tied to specific apparitions, cultural devotions, or regional devotions :

- Our Lady of Guadalupe (Mexico)

- Virgen de los Ángeles (Costa Rica)

- La Negrita (Costa Rica)

- Our Lady of Fatima (Portugal)

- Our Lady of Lourdes (France)

- Our Lady of Czestochowa (Poland)

- Our Lady of Prompt Succor (New Orleans, USA) — invoked for quick aid and protection

- Our Lady of Solitude (Nuestra Señora de la Soledad) — observed during Holy Week in Spanish-speaking regions

- Our Lady of Arabia — patroness of the Arabian Peninsula, venerated in Kuwait and Bahrain

- Our Lady of Los Remedios — venerable in Spain and Latin America as a symbol of healing and protection

- Queen of Poland — a deeply cherished patriotic devotion

- Our Lady of Sorrows

And many more — every region and culture speaks to her through unique titles, such as Our Lady of Peace, of the Rosary, of Abundance, of Good Counsel, of Prompt Succor, of Perpetual Help, of Charity, and countless localized invocations .

Christian Ancestors & Spiritual Lineage

Christianity — and especially the Black church — has always been a cornerstone of Hoodoo. Even if someone today identifies as a full-blown atheist, within Southern and Black American culture there are sayings and expressions that carry the echo of faith that can be uttered. People still call on Jesus, sometimes consciously and sometimes simply because it's embedded in the language passed down through generations. A stubbed toe might be met with "Oh Jesus!" A long, weary day might bring out, "Lord, have mercy." Whether meant literally or habitually, these words carry the living current of our shared history.

That history exists because so many of us who practice Hoodoo have Christian ancestors. As an American tradition, Hoodoo has always been influenced by the dominant religion of the land — and in the United States, that religion has been Christianity. Christian ancestors show up in our work whether they were truly devout or not. Some wore the veil of Christianity as a necessity for survival, syncretizing their African beliefs and spirits beneath the cover of the cross. Others were sincere Christians who lived by the Gospel, prayed over their families, and wove their faith into every part of life.

In my own lineage, I have known very Christian ancestors who viewed the Bible as both allegorical and mystical, holding truth in story and in symbol. They saw scripture as a living text that could guide life and open the way for divine intervention. And it was through ancestral contact that the rosary — and eventually the Hoodoo Rosary — entered my practice.

One of my Christian ancestors, a man who presents as a Franciscan, encouraged me to continue the 'family practice" of working the Psalms by first introducing me to the tradition of Scottish Psalm singing. Most recently, he encouraged me to deepen my prayer life by learning the rosary prayers in Latin, helping me connect and feel the prayers more deeply.

He showed me how psalm work could live not only in traditional Hoodoo forms like speaking them over floor washes or reciting them in chants and songs, but also in the meditative rhythm of bead-by-bead prayer.

When I pray the rosary deeply, I often slip into a trance. My fingers move steadily bead to bead but I feel myself transported — praying alongside my ancestors who once prayed these same words. The sound current, the physical act of the beads moving through my hands, and the meditations all create a space where I know I am not praying alone.

In my case, this was a direct, bloodline ancestor who drew me into conscious connection between Hoodoo and the rosary. But the rosary can also connect you to saints and other spirits tied to your lineage of devotion especially if you are using specific chaplets like:

- A St. Anne Chaplet for those devoted to the mother of Mary.

- A St. Expedite Chaplet to connect to St. Expedite.

- A St. Michael Rosary for connecting to the Archangel of protection and the celestial choirs of angels.

No matter which form of rosary or chaplet you choose, I have found that praying the Hail Mary as a devotional act strengthens ancestral work. Marian devotion itself has deepened my connection to my ancestors in ways I could never have predicted. I sometimes pray other petitions on the Hail Mary beads and see results, but I've learned that regularly offering the traditional rosary to Mary is like giving her a bouquet of flowers—something she has expressed her love for through various apparitions. St. Louis de Montfort even described visions where each Hail Mary was like a literal rose offered to the Virgin Mary, a beautiful reminder of how much she treasures this devotion.

In return, she grants spiritual graces. For me, one of those graces has been an even stronger link to my ancestral work. Through Marian devotion, I have received not only blessings for my life now but also a deeper, living relationship with the spirits of my bloodline.

Notes: Ways to Identify and Connect with Christian Ancestors

Even if you don't know their names, you can still locate and work with the Christian ancestors in your lineage. Use these clues and practices to help you connect:

Signs You Have Christian Ancestors:

- Family heirlooms such as worn Bibles, rosaries, church fans, hymnals, or Sunday hats.

- Old photos taken outside of churches or in formal Sunday dress.

- Family sayings or blessings that reference Jesus, the Lord, or Bible verses.

- Gospel or hymn melodies that feel familiar even if you've never learned them.

- A strong, unexplained pull toward Christian symbols, psalms, or churches.

***

Ways to Connect:

1. Altar Work: Place a Bible, rosary, cross, or church candle on your ancestor altar.

2. Hymn or Psalm Singing: Sing the hymns or psalms they may have loved, even if only from memory or recordings.

3. Rosary Prayer: Invite them to join you as you pray; speak their names before you begin.

4. Shared Scripture: Read aloud their favorite scripture or psalm, and ask them to guide you in understanding its deeper meaning.

5. Offerings: Offer the foods they enjoyed after church, such as coffee, tea, pound cake, or Sunday dinner dishes. (If you can't leave food out nor have an altar you can still eat it in their honor and offer the first bite to be enjoyed alongside you)

6. Syncretic Recognition: Acknowledge both their public faith and any hidden practices they may have carried alongside it.

Tip: Working with Christian ancestors can be especially powerful on Sundays, feast days of saints they loved, or during church service hours — even if you're not in the pews yourself.

Frequently Asked Questions About the Rosary

Do I need to be Catholic to pray the rosary?

Absolutely not. You do not need to be Catholic—or even Christian—to have a relationship with Mary. Growing a connection to Mary will not automatically make you a Catholic, nor will it suddenly make you fall in love with a white, long-haired Jesus from religious paintings. There is a popular Catholic saying: "To Christ through Mary." In my experience, this doesn't mean you'll wake up one day as a conservative churchgoer. What it does mean is that you will be Christed—anointed, made holy, made magical—through your relationship with her. Mary reshapes you. She purifies and empowers. But she does not erase your identity, path, or freedom.

What if I don't believe everything in the Creed?

That's completely fine. Many mystics and seekers wrestle with parts of the Creed. If you don't wish to say it, you can choose a rosary with a medal or alternate beginning so you don't feel you are "skipping" anything. Keep in mind, though, that reciting the Creed can sometimes deepen your connection with ancestors who did believe in it. It can act as a bridge between your devotion and theirs.

Can I have a relationship with Mary and other deities?

Yes. Mary is not territorial in the way that some gods and goddesses can be. I personally do not invite her into workings with deities whose energy clashes with hers (for example, I would not pair her with Hekate in the same working). But I do find resonance between Mary and other divine mothers such as Isis, Sophia, and Yemaya. If you feel jealousy or conflict arising in your practice, that is a cue to step back and discern what you want to prioritize.

Is it better to pray in Latin?

Praying in Latin holds a sacred power in Catholic tradition. For me personally, it was my ancestor who told me to pray in Latin, and I honor that. Praying in a "foreign" tongue also helps me enter trance more easily, since I'm not distracted by the everyday meaning of the words. At the same time, many of our African American ancestors were never taught prayers in Latin. English—or your heart language—is perfectly valid. Choose what deepens your devotion.

Do I have to pray the whole rosary at once?

Not at all. You can pray a single decade, a few Hail Marys, or the full five decades. The beads are a tool, not a chain. Mary hears every prayer, whether long or short. That said, setting aside time for a full rosary can strengthen the spiritual "muscles" of focus, stillness, and surrender.

Will praying the rosary make me a stronger manifester or magician?

Yes. The rosary trains your concentration, visualization, and discipline—all crucial magical skills. It forces you to slow down, enter meditation, and put your will into rhythm with Spirit. Stepping away from distractions and touching something real (the beads) roots your prayer in both body and spirit. Many mystics say the most formidable "Christian magicians" are not theologians but ordinary women and men who pray the rosary faithfully.

Is the rosary good for fighting addiction?

Yes. Countless saints, mystics, and even modern Catholic voices testify to its power against addiction, especially pornography. Many say it is impossible to keep both a daily rosary practice and an active addiction—you will eventually choose one or the other.

In my own life, I used to be an emotional eater. Since committing to the rosary, I've found much greater control over my urges. My time feels holier, my interests more pure. The rosary makes you steward your life better—your appetites, your energy, and your time.

Why do Catholics sometimes talk about praying the rosary as if it were an act of violence?

In some circles, the rosary is spoken of as a "weapon" against unwanted cultural change or against people considered "enemies." You may hear it invoked in nationalist ways, as if Mary were blessing a crusade.

I believe the Mary they invoke is not the Mary I know. Just as it's been said that "the master and the slave cannot worship the same God," I believe the oppressor and the oppressed cannot be invoking the same Mary.

Yes, Padre Pio called the rosary "the weapon of our time." But the weapon is not for domination or conquest—it is for spiritual defense, for healing, for protection. Mary does not call down bombs or bloodshed. She appears before violence, offering warning, refuge, and peace.

The rosary I know is not for hate, but for love. Not for division, but for communion. Not for destruction, but for true justice.

Do I have to be African American to use the Hoodoo Rosary? Can I still pray it if I'm not African American?

Anyone can pray the rosary, no matter their race and no matter their religion. The rosary is prayer, and prayer is open to every soul who comes with humility and sincerity.

When people say that Hoodoo is a closed practice, they are usually speaking about the ways it draws from the lived experiences, cultural memory, and the blessings of African American ancestors. Naturally, your own ancestors will bless you more deeply than they will bless an outsider, because they are your family. The same principle applies here: if you are praying the Hoodoo Rosary with a heart that honors your own line and shows respect to Mary, the saints, and the spirits, you will be heard.

But if you come to the rosary as something to steal or strip for power—without reverence, without relationship—you may find little fruit. It is less a question of race than it is of respect. Working with any spirit, whether ancestors, saints, angels, or Mary herself, requires reverence, knowledge of their stories, and gratitude for their presence. Approaching as a colonizer—seeking to pillage blessings without giving honor—closes the door. Approaching with love, reverence, and the willingness to learn opens it.

The Hoodoo Rosary, like any true devotion, responds to sincerity. It will not reward taking, but it will bless giving.

Will praying the Rosary limit my ability to connect to God on my own? Will it be like going backwards?

No. The rosary is not meant to limit your relationship with God—it is meant to deepen it. The rosary teaches you how to have a devotional practice and strengthens your relationship with the Divine. Mary never asks for worship; she always points back to God, whether you call God, Allah, the Divine or the God within you.

The rosary is simply a spiritual practice, one of many you can incorporate into your life, and it should enhance rather than take away from your prayer life. Many who develop a relationship with Mary find themselves even closer to God, to Christ within themselves, and to the Holy Spirit. Mary acts as an ally who helps open the heart to God's presence.

In my own life, Mary and Archangel Michael are the only beings within the Christian tradition who have revealed themselves to me vividly—both in dreams and beyond them. They have never led me away from God; they have only brought me closer. Through the rosary, my connection with God has grown stronger, my spiritual abilities have increased, and I have experienced more of the gifts of the Holy Spirit.

That said, if the rosary feels uncomfortable for you, it may not be your path—and that is okay. But rest assured that those who have a true relationship with Mary through the rosary are drawn nearer to God, not further away, and often find their gifts, faith, and spiritual clarity multiplied.

Anielle Reid is a mystic, author, and rootworker devoted to helping seekers connect with their true spiritual power. She first introduced her work to the world through T*he Magick and Mediums Oracle*, a visionary deck that opened doors for countless people to explore their intuition and spiritual gifts. Since then, she has created *The Slavic Oracle, The Golden Light Oracle*, and *The Latin Love Oracle*, each offering unique pathways to ancestral wisdom and sacred connection.

As an author, Anielle expanded her devotion to prayer and mysticism with *The People's Rosary*, a groundbreaking guide that reframed the rosary for modern seekers and mystics. With *The Hoodoo Rosary*, she continues her mission of blending devotion and conjure, showing how prayer beads can become a living tool for magic, healing, and transformation.

Passionate about connecting people to their ancestral magic, Anielle teaches that every soul has access to divine strength, guidance, and protection. Her work encourages readers to honor their ancestors, trust their inner wisdom, and cultivate authentic spirituality that celebrates both heritage and personal power.

Through her books, decks, and teachings, Anielle invites you to step into a deeper relationship with your guides, your God, and yourself—and to discover the infinite possibilities of grace and magic.

www.ingramcontent.com/pod-product-compliance
Lightning Source LLC
Chambersburg PA
CBHW071235070526
44583CB00017B/2192